All the
SONNETS
of
SHAKESPEARE

Bestselling title, *All the Sonnets of Shakespeare* is now available in audiobook form, read by Kenneth Branagh and Lolita Chakrabarti.

The audiobook can be downloaded from Audible, Nook, Scribd and Google Play.

'This new arrangement of Shakespeare's sonnets is a revelation. Paul Edmondson, and Stanley Wells have truly illuminated the author's themes, preoccupations and obsessions. In so doing the poems have a fresh, and startlingly clear narrative progression. Thanks to their scholarship I found myself experiencing this work as never before. There is a directness, simplicity, and humanity, which shines from the page. It was an honour to read them in this form. I hope a large audience will enjoy seeing (and hearing), this new light shone on a great literary treasure.'

KENNETH BRANAGH

Discover audiobooks from Cambridge at www.cambridge.org/audiobooks

CAMBRIDGE
UNIVERSITY PRESS

GRANTA

12 Addison Avenue, London W11 4QR | email: editorial@granta.com
To subscribe visit subscribe.granta.com, or call +44 (0) 1371 851873

ISSUE 158: WINTER 2022

DEPARTMENT FOR
CONTINUING
EDUCATION

UNIVERSITY OF
OXFORD

Part-time courses in
Creative Writing and Literature

Short courses – in Oxford and online
Day and weekend events, weekly classes
and summer schools.

Part-time Oxford qualifications
Undergraduate certificates and diplomas
Postgraduate degrees
Apply now for autumn 2022 entry

@OxfordConted   **www.conted.ox.ac.uk/granta2022**

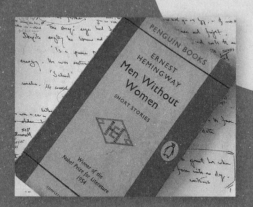

CONTENTS

Introduction

Writer Fatima Bhutto, daughter of politician Murtaza Bhutto (who was assassinated in 1996), niece of Benazir Bhutto (assassinated in 2007), is in lockdown in rural England. Her Jack Russell, Coco, is about to give birth, and the signs are not good. After a long wait, a malformed puppy is delivered stillborn, and Coco, unhinged in grief, adopts the author's hand instead, licking it red and raw. We can only speculate about her consciousness, but call it what you will – desperate maternal delusion or instinct – in Coco's mind a hand is now an approximation of a puppy. A body part, like Gogol's nose, has been brought to independent life. 'The Hour of the Wolf' is a personal meditation on grief, and the prehistoric bond between dogs and humans. It has a slightly uncanny quality, a sense of proportions slightly out of kilter, which is to do with the pandemic, or rather with lockdown. I don't think we have quite processed yet what those months of isolation did to us – a time of fear and daily death tolls and also of unprecedented curtailment of our freedom of movement. But there were consolations. Those of us lucky enough to have dogs by our side learned to better read their expressions and body language as they learned to read ours, a conversation between two species evolving together over the millennia.

Oliver Sacks would have been interested in Coco's delusion. He was a writer, but his quest to bring empathy to the diagnostic interaction – to sit with patients, listen to them, touch them, play them music, dance with them – was a way of making sense of suffering beyond language. In this issue, Will Rees describes the experience of trying to make sense of his own illness, at a time when he came close to being diagnosed with lymphoma. The narratives emerging from the doctors' notes – Rees was copied in – always lagged a few days behind the latest medical investigations, and subsequent consultations seemed never quite to take all the details and results into account. This is not a story of hypochondria – it's a story of an enquiring mind drawing its own conclusions, and then more conclusions. Does care fail if communication fails? To have pain, as Elaine Scarry wrote, is to have certainty; to hear about the pain of others is to have doubt. Rees draws attention to the complexities of medical communication, the mutual dance of patient and doctor governed, at best, by the logical steps of the diagnostic process.

T he uprisings sweeping the Arab world challenged entrenched corruption and neglect in the name of justice, accountability and human rights, until one by one they failed. Lebanon seemed a more hopeful story, but ruled by power-sharing factions the country has stumbled through a gradual, then intense, decline. Charif Majdalani described what he saw in his vivid journal *Beirut 2020: The Collapse of a Civilization, a Journal*, translated from the French by Ruth Diver. I asked him if he had more material, and he did – this sequel is a tale of a capital now virtually without electricity or fuel. The stars are bright above Beirut's blacked-out streets, and there are rumours of emaciated bears rescued from hellish cages by foreign NGOs, carried out on stretchers to safer environments. A street vendor from Syria reveals that his family is in a refugee camp in Turkey. Others have been saving to pay people smugglers; inflation has made their money worthless. Even hard-currency accounts are worth a fraction of their true value: money traders buy dollar cheques for fluctuating amounts – around some 12 per cent of their value – then sell them back to the issuing banks, who wipe the amounts off the accounts. Is it legal? What does the term even mean in this context, where corruption and factionalism are endemic, and where the landscape is scarred by money-laundering development projects and mountains of refuse? The Lebanese people, briefly uniting in the pro-democracy uprising of 2019, are now fracturing again into sectarianism and clans, keeping it all in the family. ∎

Sigrid Rausing

Courtesy of the author

THE HOUR OF THE WOLF

Fatima Bhutto

1

One day I see a wild deer. It is evening, the second month of lockdown in the first spring of the pandemic. I am outside with my pregnant dog, who is days away from delivery, her first, but it doesn't look like she is pregnant at all. Her stomach is almost concave and aside from a week when she was ravenous, her appetite is delicate and her mood strange. The vets in this Oxfordshire village where we have decamped to ride out what we imagine will be the first and only wave of this virus won't give us an appointment. *It's not an emergency*, they tell me on the phone, *we are only seeing emergencies during Covid*. No one knows what Covid is yet, none of us know how to behave. What does the virus have to do with a pregnant dog? I describe my dog's hollow stomach, the stillness when I place my hand on her belly. Once, I thought I saw something move. Another time, I thought I saw something poke out of her flank in a picture. It's not a phantom pregnancy, she's had one of those before. We had a scan, she is carrying a litter of puppies. But something doesn't feel right. *She sounds fine*, these new vets – who we don't know and have never met – tell me on the phone. We are not from here; we are far, far away from home.

9

Outside, in the garden, Coco and I both see the deer. It seems large for a deer, tall and noble, her skin reddish in the twilight. My dog is small, six kilos with the weight of her non-phantom babies. Coco descends from hunters and ratters and dives into rabbit warrens, runs up trees, she burrows and digs and pirouettes, and though she is the gentlest creature I have ever known, thrilled by the chase but never by the kill, she took a rabbit by the throat the other day. MC, who is a botanist, was thrilled. She leads dendrology tours all over the world, examining the flora and fauna of Chile, Yemen, Greece. When she's home, she tends to her heritage garden in Oxfordshire, growing deep purple irises, plump red roses, perfumed magnolia trees. Allegra – my best friend – and I have rented a portion of MC's cottage, and in the evenings of our lockdown, MC walks us through the sprawling garden to smell the perfume of the night-blooming flowers.

The rabbits eat all her rare and precious plants and we were together when Coco proudly wagged her curly tail over her dead prey, running back and forth between me and the grey rabbit's warm, twitching body, eager for praise. 'Well done, Coco,' MC cooed. I didn't praise her, but I understood. She was hunting for her babies, hunting to be sure there would be food for her young. Now, Coco glares at the wild deer, her spine arched, the hair on her neck standing on end, her lithe, balletic body trembling, ready to catch and kill the doe too.

Barry Lopez, who wrote about wild wolves in his seminal book *Of Wolves and Men*, describes the moment a hunter and its prey lock eyes. A decision is made then, Lopez says, in this moment he calls 'the conversation of death'. There is ritual in the exchange between hunter and hunted: 'the flesh of the hunted in exchange for respect for its spirit'. This tension doesn't exist in captive animals; it's bred out of them. But free animals, wild animals, obey a sacred order. One animal must kill to live, to feed the old and the young of its pack, and the other must surrender himself to protect *his* brethren, his old and young, from being taken. There is, Lopez writes in his ethnography of wolves, a dignity in this encounter – both animals, not just the predator, make a choice in this ceremony. They agree on death. 'When the wolf "asks" for the life of another animal he is responding to something in that animal that says, "My life is strong. It is worth asking for."' The nobility of this death is that it is appropriate, it is a chosen death. Not a tragedy. 'I have lived a full life, says the prey. I am ready to die. I am willing to die because clearly I will be dying so that the others in this small herd will go on living.'

My life is strong. It is worth asking for.

Chosen death. I think of my father, Murtaza. He was a politician and an MP in Pakistan. He was forty-two years old when he was killed, only four years older than I am now, but he made the decision to give his life long before that, when he was a young man, just after his own father was assassinated. My father raised me on his own, as a single father, till I was eight years old. He made our life, lived in exile during the dark days of Pakistan's dictatorship in the 1980s, a game of fun and mystery. But there would come a time, he always told me, preparing me, that they would take him too. When I cried and begged him to take his warnings back, my father would hold me and kiss me and wipe away my tears. I had to be brave, he would tell me, always smiling, it was my patrimony. He never took his warnings back. Though he loved his time on Earth, he knew that when they came to take it, he would give them his life. There was a beauty to my father, a romance to how he saw the world, no matter its cruelties. I think it came from that acceptance, what Nietzsche called amor fati, a love of one's fate. It is a radical choice not to 'merely bear what is necessary', Nietzsche wrote, 'but love it'. The brave meet death with courage, there is no other choice. But free men meet it with joy.

From my understanding of the philosopher – and who really understands Nietzsche? – this is what makes ordinary humans great: a total love and acceptance of their fate. At the time he was killed, my father was in the prime of his life, the father of a young son and teenage daughter. He had just begun his career in politics, there was promise in his future. He had so much to do and much to struggle against. But he would not have traded that giving of his life, his strong, hopeful life, for anything – not for power, not for wealth, not even for me. It was a gift, he wanted to give it. 'I should like to be able to love my country and still love justice,' Albert Camus said. My father loved both.

We know almost nothing about animals. What little we know, we can only see through a prism that reflects our own image. Ours is the purest image we know; we are thoughtlessly entranced by it. To us, there is nothing on Earth greater or grander or more sophisticated than the self, than ourselves. This is our great failure as a species. We use all our strengths, intelligence and time in pursuit of a very shallow idea – that we are special. This is an ancient idea, constantly at war with that essential truth spoken thousands of years ago by Buddha: there is no self. We are not unique and no essence of ours will remain. Ultimately, we, like everything else on Earth, are pure matter, dust. It is how we are born and how we will end, absorbed into the earth and forgotten.

Coco is no wolf, no saviour, no prince among men. She is a Jack Russell terrier, the size and hysteria of a mongoose, at best. She has no chance against a deer, a centaur compared to her tiny frame. But she doesn't know that. She is lit by a primal confidence, a natural stalker enlivened by the scent of a beautiful adversary. MC, the botanist, tells me later that the deer, who also devour her plants, are muntjacs, and that they have come to Oxfordshire from China, introduced in the early twentieth century. But escapes and releases of muntjacs into the wild have resulted in feral populations running loose across England.

Coco holds the deer's gaze for five seconds and then, conversation exchanged, leaps at it, heart pounding, racing, running to be joined in ceremony. But the deer escapes. It doesn't jump over the garden fence, it doesn't hit the brick and mortar of the home, it just disappears, vanishes. We never see it again.

2

Coco has been with me since she was three months old. I bought her as a gift for my youngest brother and then, in the two nights that it took to vaccinate her and fly her home to Pakistan, fell in love with her. He had asked for a girl dog, named her after a Japanese cartoon character, even decided where she would sleep – with him, at the foot of his bed. By the time we reached Karachi, I was already thinking how best to break the bad news to a ten-year-old boy. But immediately after meeting my little brother, Coco growled at him, snarling, showing off her sharp little teeth. 'The good news is I bought a dog,' I told him warmly. 'The bad news is that she's mine.'

I felt no guilt over it; by day three, Coco was bonded to me and I to her. It turned out for the best. As a matter of principle, Coco hates children. She isn't fond of other people or dogs either. As a pup she barked at strangers on the road, incensed that others might walk on the very street she was using. When she doesn't like someone (this is often), she has been known to yap tirelessly at them until they go away. She is exceedingly bright and loving to a select few, but putting it mildly, she is a character. To me, she is perfect, and over our years together, has been faithful, constantly watching over me.

Though I have had dogs all my life, Coco is my first real companion. I cared for her and she for me at a point when I was figuring out how to live, how to remake a world of my own, alone. In those lonely years, Coco and I travelled continents together and set up quiet lives. As anxious as I was, as uncertain of how to build a small corner for myself, I somehow managed to care for this dog and she not only survived, she grew, she learned, she adapted and even thrived. A model writer's dog, she sits quietly while I work, holding a ball in between her paws, her body tensed but patient for hours. Always cautious, Coco turns to look at me in the park when she spots a pigeon – *shall we chase him?* – awaiting approval and confirmation that this is something I'd like her to do on our behalf. The times I have gotten angry at

Coco are when she has behaved like an animal, running across traffic in chase of a cat without checking with me first, overturning the garbage, jumping on the kitchen table to eat all the food or kicking off her nappy when she's on heat to smear blood all over the floor in decorative trails. I get angry because I know I cannot protect her in her world, the animal world, but only in mine.

At night, my dog burrows under the covers of my bed. Only once she has rooted and rustled, sleeping for a while in the den-like dark under the blankets, does she slowly drift up until she is on the pillow and we are nose to nose. When I hold her and stroke her, telling her how clever she is, how pretty, how good, she closes her eyes and sighs, breathing softly. When I am working and her store of patience has finally run out, she jumps up to my lap and rests her warm throat in the crook of my elbow so I cannot write or type. We have been through scares, heartbreaks, stayed in hotel rooms in strange cities, boarded planes and boats and trains, learned tricks, lost people, been betrayed. There has been so much life in this little time. Only six years.

I wanted her to have a litter of puppies because it was essential for her health and general life experience. It wasn't because I wanted children, was desperate for my own, and could do nothing about it. It would be good for her, becoming a mother, good for me too, good for us, I said. It would be good for us.

Forty kilometres from Kathmandu is Namo Buddha. The road there is choppy, bumpy, choked with the smog of scooters and trucks and jeeps, some with stickers of Prince Siddhartha, cross-legged and serene, plastered on their rear windows. It is there, at the Namo Buddha stupa, that Buddha encountered a starving tigress and fed her of his own flesh.

The tigress, her body hollowed and drooping, was close to death. Already her cubs had no food; when she died, they would too. Overcome with compassion, Buddha gives himself to her, feeding the tigress his body so that she may eat and her cubs survive. I travelled to Namo Buddha some years ago, alone, with a guide. The tigers have all gone now, there are barely any left in the Nepalese wild, just over 200. I went to the stupa, a dusty mound, away from the oxblood walls of the Thrangu Tashi Yangtse Monastery where young boys with shaved heads chant prayers. There was no one there, save an old lady selling amulets on a rickety table.

It was on that journey to Nepal that I first became enchanted with the wild. In Chitwan, days earlier, we had tracked the vanished tigers – seen their claw marks on the bark of aged trees, smelled their scent – but never seen them. We trekked into the jungle at dawn, at dusk, on foot, in cars. I went birdwatching, and bathed a wounded elephant. I had never been so close to the living world before, never so transfixed. I was lonely; being close to the wild comforted me, soothed me. Ecclesiastes tells us that 'dark is the wilderness', the wild a place no one can see God. But God is everywhere in the wilderness. If God is not there, in the mist that travels through a forest at dawn, in the dew that nourishes the soil, in the delicate birds and scavengers, then where is God?

It was in a deer park that Buddha gave his first sermon. And there, among the monks as Buddha expounded the four noble truths, 'I teach suffering – its origin, cessation and path. That is all I teach,' was a doe, listening.

3

Coco's due date came and went. She had mated twice but counting from the second time, she was still late. Her stomach never grew though she became sluggish and her energy sunk to nothing. Dogs, like humans, have morning sickness, throwing up yellow bile and suffering fluctuations in appetite. I clung to the fact that Coco had experienced both these things. A phone call to a vet in London raised my alarms, she should absolutely be checked they insisted. The Oxfordshire vets begrudgingly consented and so, in masks and gloves, I brought Coco for a check-up.

No humans were allowed into the clinic, Covid protocols were still new and strange and Coco was taken from the car kicking and screaming. She returned twenty minutes later, leaping, desperate to escape the vet, who told me from a distance that yes, she was fine, he saw the pups. Two of them, heads and spines growing nicely. It should be any day now. When I told friends who knew something of the world of dogs, they went quiet. *Only two puppies?* they asked. *Are you sure?* I had always felt something wasn't right. But I had read the books and prepared the whelping box and bought the vet-bed fleece and had forceps and scales, calcium and glucose, everything that I could possibly need. I wrote out a list of warning signs for the two friends I was with in case the delivery happened while I was out running.

Allegra, an Italian writer, and I have been best friends for over fifteen years now. I was staying with her when I bought Coco. *Allegra, I texted her, having forgotten to mention I was getting a dog, would it be OK if I brought a dog home? Just for two nights?* Allegra's home is beautiful, furnished with exquisite taste, not a cushion out of place. Ever generous, Allegra consented, sounding only a little worried. When she came home that evening and saw a little pup dancing on her vintage carpet, she smiled and asked me to make sure I washed her feet and my hands every time we returned from the outside. She liked Coco but didn't particularly want her on her bed or sitting on the chairs around the dining table. Allegra's caution lasted about a day. Today, they go walking for hours in the park. Allegra mushes up dog food with her fingers and sings Coco good-morning songs and buys her treats, hiding them in her room so when they are curled up together, on the bed where Coco sprawls luxuriantly, paws unwashed, Allegra can feed her one, two or three, as she whispers praise while stroking the patterned crown on Coco's head.

I read the emergency list to Allegra and MC at lunch and dinner.
Pain is normal, dogs tear at their bedding during labour.
Blood should be expected, normal.
Green discharge before any puppies arrive is not normal – a vet should be called immediately; it means something is seriously wrong.

Green discharge after a puppy or in between puppies, however, is fine. Normal.

Anything longer than twenty minutes of consistent pushing could be bad though there can be up to three hours of waiting time between each pup.

They know the danger signs by heart. Everyone in our little lockdown bubble is prepared.

4

Coco's labour began on a Monday morning. Lazing in her whelping box, snoozing in a sliver of early spring sun, she started, jumping up and yelping. The contractions had begun. After she recovered from the shock, Coco scuttled around the bed in anxious circles, biting the blanket, pulling at it with her teeth and shredding it with her paws. I called the vet, they told me to be patient, most births happened in the middle of the night. I confirmed their emergency number. They told me they'd talk to me the next morning, but I confirmed it anyway. The day passed slowly. Coco nibbled at her food and sat in my lap. We went to sleep. I lay on the bed facing her whelping box, listening to her breathe in the dark.

Just after midnight, Coco woke me up crying. She wanted to go outside and was whimpering, running around in circles, looking distressed. Foggily, I put on my boots and turned on the light as we ran down the stairs. I clipped on her leash – the books said dogs burrow under hedges, seeking privacy and quiet when they're ready to deliver – and we ran out the door. Back inside, Coco trotted back up the stairs. I was still woozy with sleep when we entered the bedroom and I saw the marks on the carpet, small curlicues of wispy stains. I bent down and looked, blinking to make sure. They were green.

I am not a naturalist, not a biologist, not an environmentalist. I don't know anything about animals except that I care for them and have grown up around dogs. Sometimes there were also cats, horses, rats, small rodents, birds and deer. There are raging debates about whether we should or should not anthropomorphise animals. Frans de Waal, the famous primatologist, dismisses the strange, distancing language that's commonly used among those who study animals. A kiss is not a kiss but 'mouth-to-mouth contact', animals that have fought and made up don't reconcile but engage in 'post-conflict behaviour', weirdest is 'vocalised panting' – scrubbed of anything that might actually remind us of laughter. De Waal calls this non-human terminology 'linguistic castration'.

In one book, de Waal tells us that when writing of chimps, he uses 'animals' only for simplicity's sake. He would prefer to say 'non-human animals' because, after all, we are animals too. All this to say, I don't know what the correct terminology is and I don't know how one is supposed to talk about the wild, the free, or even the captive and domesticated. I don't know what I am allowed to suppose or imagine. But that night, crouching on the carpet, looking at Coco through the dim, orange glow of the bedroom light, I could see that she was scared.

The next hour moved quickly, I called the vet's emergency number, MC put her boots on and got the car out while Allegra helped me put Coco into a laundry basket, panting loudly, her svelte stomach visibly contracting and releasing. We drove to the clinic and again, because of Covid protocols, I was not allowed inside. The young doctor who had told me we were expecting two puppies took Coco's basket from me and told us to wait in the car.

The labour was complicated, he said when he reappeared half an hour later. Coco was a first-time mother and nervous. First, he suggested keeping her in the clinic so he could observe her. Then another half hour later, he said she might be delaying labour out of anxiety and that we should take her home and come back if there was no delivery by 4 a.m. It was close to 2 a.m. by the time we were driving back to the cottage. And just as we pulled into the driveway, the birth began. Coco started to pace within the cramped laundry basket, biting the edges, pushing with her whole body. I could see that the pup was in breach, coming out legs first. The iron scent of blood filled the air.

In the dark light of MC's car, aided by my camera flashlight, I had tried to film her, half in celebration and half to send to the vet, when I noticed that something was wrong. For all her straining, the puppy wasn't being pushed out. 'Take her basket into the house,' the vet advised on the phone, 'you'll have to deliver the puppies, slowly easing them out in tandem with her breathing, gently, as she exhales.' Upstairs, in a better-lit room, I crouched on the floor close to Coco and whispered to her as I brought my hand towards her – without air the pup couldn't survive, she had to deliver him soon. But as my fingers touched its wet, curled body, I felt bone but no flesh. There were legs, but no underside, no stomach, no chest. The puppy was mangled, just hollowed out blood and bone.

Dogs sometimes pull at their pups, yanking the gelatinous amniotic sac and biting the umbilical cord as they are being delivered. In the panic and the pain, could she have eaten her baby? I didn't see her do it. We got back in the car and drove through the night to the clinic once more. Spiriting Coco away again, the vet returned and told us that the puppy was malformed. There were not, it turned out, two pups but just one. The puppy had no body and an oversized head, it was already dead. Because of its enlarged head, Coco would have to have a Caesarean to expel the body. In the parking lot, I was given a form to sign acknowledging that my dog may not survive, and that any liability and loss would be my own.

Over the course of my life, I have lost nearly all my family members to violent deaths. I was a fourteen-year-old girl, at home when my father was assassinated outside the house. I mention this not to posit any equivalence between the two events, but only to say that I didn't need to sign a form. I knew the loss would be my own.

Coco came home shortly afterwards. No Caesarean. She delivered her lifeless puppy and the vet, shaken by the experience, finally let me inside the clinic. Coco scrambled to get outside, away from him, from there, from everything. And for a moment, I thought she seemed fine, normal. She won't remember this, my friends reassured me. They don't feel the way we do. They're different. But that night, trembling non-stop, Coco slept in my bed moaning, howling.

5

When a dog has given birth to a litter of puppies, she presides over them fully. Her stomach sheds hair so that they can suckle more easily; she is their only source of food and nourishment for a month. She warms her young with her body and licks them in order to stimulate urination and defecation. If a mother rejects her pups, this stimulation has to be done by a human, with cotton and warm water, otherwise the newborn puppies can't expel waste. For the week after her stillbirth, Coco refused to leave my bed, clinging to me, shivering constantly. She growled and barked hysterically if anyone came into the room or approached us when we were together, even Allegra, whom she has loved since her own puppyhood. Her appetite vanished, eating only what I ate if anything at all, lifting her head from my lap long enough to take the food from my fingers, settling her head back down to chew.

Initially, I assumed Coco was licking my hand for comfort. She would start with the back, licking until my skin was pink and raw, and then flip it around to lick my palm. But then she started sleeping on my hand, holding it, caressing it, jumping to it whenever anyone opened the door or she heard voices approaching us. It was motherhood, her instincts alert and alive; she would be a mother even with no child. It was more than motherhood, it was grief.

I have been a student of grief my whole life but I had never seen anything like this primal mourning. Animals were supposed to be different from us, they were supposed to forget. I submitted my hand to Coco day after day until the vet – still unable to explain to me how he had had no clue that something had been wrong with no enlarged stomach, no pregnancy weight gain, no prenatal kicking and squirming or even how he had seen two heads and two hearts instead of one, or none – told me that Coco wouldn't heal if she thought my hand was a child. Her body would keep producing milk and her hormones would be firing away, reacting to all her postnatal needs. I had felt her clammy body as she hung on to me. I thought it was sweat, warmth from the sheets and the heating.

You have to take your hand away from her, the vet cautioned. I tried, but failed many times. She had lost her child. I gave her my hand. If anyone came into the room, between frantic barks Coco would lower her face, licking the skin of my hand, her eyes level with the intruder, sparkling with terror, and her low voice humming somewhere between a whimper and a snarl.

If the covenant between animal and man is as old as time, the first domesticated dog appearing between 20,000 and 40,000 years ago, why does it feel outlandish to speak of the bonds between us? A small voice drums it into my head that I am a serious writer (or at least, I think I am supposed to be a serious writer, I have no idea what I really am), how can I talk about love and loneliness and suffering in the kingdom of animal and man?

In the spring of the first lockdown, animals inherit the earth. Pigeons, normally skittish, no longer scare and flutter away when you run past them in the street. They stare at you. *Why are you here? Why have you come back?* On a farm in the English countryside, where another of my friends has decamped during quarantine, a cow becomes ill. Her bones protrude from her skin and the farmers decide that there's no other course of action; she will have to be put down. They shoot her in the field, in view of all the other cows, who erupt in a procession of mooing. They moo all night, my friend says, keening in mourning. At four in the morning, after a brief pause, they begin their grieving anew. The cow's calf is among the grieving herd, she saw her mother die. They don't stop mooing for two days.

My memory is fuzzy because of all the time I am spending online, flicking through photos and tweets, trying not to think of the virus that is ravaging the planet. I don't realise it at the time but I am expending all my energy trying not to feel anything – not to feel scared about what this virus will have broken in our lives before it passes, not to feel lonely, suddenly cut off from the world. I do this so well that I don't feel anything at all. Every day repeats. I wake up, I read, I am deadlocked – I can't write. I try but I'm stuck. I need to move, to meet people, to have experiences, to be free. But these are all excuses. 'Does there not pass over man a space of time when his life is a blank?' the Koran asks.

The truth is I just can't do it. I don't want to. I tell myself that this is fine, it is normal. I don't have to write or be productive or have answers. I have to close my eyes to remember one day from another, everything feels the same: empty. On the internet, which is where I live now, I see a video of stingrays floating in the sea, their pectoral fins breaking the water as they glide under the waves. A group of stingrays is called a fever.

In a world of excess and power and all its rot, what besides love forces us to be pure? I have no feeling during the year of lockdown but some things bring me immediately to tears. Shaheed Aitzaz Hasan Bangash was a young Pakistani schoolboy who stopped a suicide bomber from entering his school, where 2,000 students could have been killed. When he saw the bomber, Aitzaz ran forward to him and embraced him with his own body, pushing him back, away from the school. Aitzaz was in the ninth grade when he gave his life to save others. He was fifteen years old. I want you to know Aitzaz Hasan's name, so that you will remember him and carry him in your heart. I call this young man Shaheed, it means martyr. We call him a martyr because he gave his life so others could see. I recite the names of our brave and defiant every day like a rosary. I carry their names with me everywhere. On the anniversaries of this boy's death, when I see his picture, I weep.

Since I am always online, checking my Twitter in the middle of the night, looking at Instagram until I know an embarrassing amount about utter strangers, I have posted a bit about animal cruelty, about failures of compassion. I follow a few shelters in Pakistan and now I am deluged with heart-stopping videos and pictures of the dark things men do to animals. Torture, abuse, abandonment, dogs burnt alive, donkeys tied up to lamp posts and hit with cars, too many pictures, too many things. It hurts me deep inside, deep beyond the unfeeling place, every time I see one of those images.

Gloria a los manos que trabajan, the Puerto Rican poet and anti-imperialist activist Juan Antonio Corretjer wrote, glory to the hands that work. The thought of migrant workers on deadly marches from cities to rural homes where they will lockdown and their families starve; the sobs of farmers who are forced to throw entire harvests away due to government price gouging, prison populations laid waste by the virus, haunts every day of this interminable year. In January, in the second year of the pandemic, which still feels very much like the first year, gunmen enter a coal mine near the town of Mach, Balochistan, and identify eleven ethnic Hazaras. The Hazara people are Shias and very distinct looking, beautiful, you can spot them in a crowd, just like the gunmen did. They marched the men out of the mine, took them to a mountaintop and killed them. After their murder, their families sat in the bitter cold and grieved, waiting for the prime minister to come and mourn with them, to promise them justice, to bring back hope from the dead. But the prime minister of Pakistan was busy meeting YouTubers and Turkish television producers. He wouldn't come.

The mourners defied Islamic convention and refused to bury their dead, holding fast to the bodies of their loved ones, waiting. But still, the prime minister refused. To the desolate poor, sitting shiva in the long winter nights, Imran Khan, the prime minister, hissed that he would not be blackmailed. What state is this where the people are the enemy and the crown is only moved by celebrity and flattery? Every voice in my head berates me – why aren't you writing about this? Why aren't you writing about serious things?

'What kind of times are these,' Brecht asked, 'in which / A conversation about trees is almost a crime / For in doing so we maintain our silence about so much wrongdoing'. The voices reprimand me. Why are you sitting in the middle of nowhere – in gardens and forests with dogs – and writing about animals? Explain yourself. Be true.

When my brother, Zulfikar, was young, we had a deer, Bambi, a fawn, that through a series of events had come to live in our garden. The deer ate leaves from the palms of our hands. When Zulfi walked in the garden talking to the champa trees and flowers, the fawn shadowed him everywhere. She loved him the way that a boy needs to be loved, softly. Never imposing or intruding, but always near him. One day, Zulfi's mother, tired of the damage done to her plants, sent the deer away, donating Bambi to the Karachi Zoo. I don't remember why we didn't know and why we couldn't stop her. I remember how upset my brother was, how painfully hurt. He rescued bats that flew into the bright, reflective glass of our dining-room window, treated birds with injured wings, and cried, sobbed, when animals were hurt in films. The zoo called us soon after, the deer – perfectly healthy – had died. Just like that, one day, out of nowhere. She died of a broken heart, they said.

I had a dog, Lama, a long-haired dachshund, who loved me more than I was able to love back. I loved her but I was afraid. I hid from her sometimes because it overwhelmed me how much she needed me. First, I was close to her and she would sleep every night in my bed, and then I was not, travelling for work and life and making my distance away from home greater and greater. To ease the heartsickness of that necessary distance, I retreated from my Karachi friends and my old life. When I came home from my trips, I wouldn't call anyone for weeks, sitting alone in my room and working. When I travelled I didn't keep in touch. I was preparing to leave my family home, but I didn't know how, and at times, I was unkind. One night, I arrived from the airport late and went straight to the annexe where I lived. In the dark cold of my bedroom, the air conditioner on full blast, I was unpacking when I heard Lama scratching at the door. She heard the car, she felt me return. I listened, even as she whimpered for me, but I didn't let her in that night.

She died three months later when I was away again. I don't forgive myself for my coldness to her. When she died, I was inconsolable, though I had been so unfeeling to Lama when I was trying to cut my ties to home. I knew I had not been good to her, not been just, and now I would have no way to redeem myself. I cried for her, for what that rejection must do to an animal whose heart is so large, and for me, ashamed that I was capable of such pettiness. *Lama hasn't gone*, my best, most beloved friend told me, *you have a bond together* – he didn't know what I had done – *and that bond means she will return to you in some form or another. Watch for it. Wait for her.*

I didn't believe him. But nine months later I got Coco. Do I feel something returned in her? I do. It is a full, large-hearted, forgiving love. I don't want to let it down this time. Not this time, not ever again. What, I ask myself over and over, do we owe the wild? It is a question that has started to haunt me, even as I know the answer. What do we owe the wild? Everything. Much more than we are willing to give, at least. ■

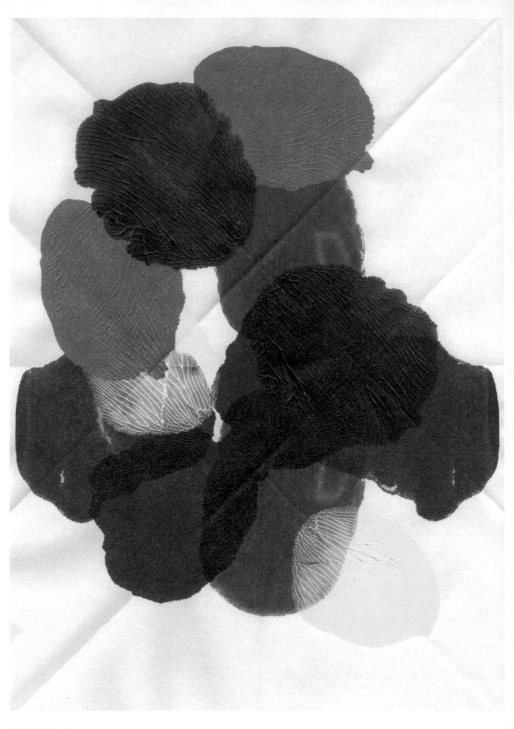

DANIEL EATOCK
Reflectasymmetric, 2019

PURE COLOUR

Sheila Heti

She doesn't know how to think about her father's death, or even if she should, or how to explain the great joy and calm that settled in her the moment the life left his body, and she felt his spirit enter her, and fill her up with joy and light. There was a moment when there was nothing, no life in him left, then the spirit that had been in her father entered her. It came in through her chest and she felt it there in her entire body – near the top of her skull, down in her toes, swirling wonderfully inside her, and the peace she knew after it settled inside her was the cleanest feeling of love; a brightness that finally compelled her to sit up, having felt it swirling long enough that now it seemed time to share it, to go downstairs and hug her uncle, and tell him, *Dad is dead*, and to try and hug him close enough that maybe he could feel it, too; her father's love that was streaming through her. So complete was the feeling of peace and joy, and relief for her father that it was all done, the difficult endeavour that had been his life, and the carrying of all that was heavy – it was over, and out of the deflation of his body came the purest joy. Then, maybe twenty minutes later, such a deep chill came over her, and her teeth started chattering, and they would not stop clacking together, and her arms were freezing up, and her entire body was freezing and chattering, so that she returned back upstairs to her father's body and sat beside him in his bed, and pulled the covers up, not even looking at him, but trying to warm her body there. Had his spirit left her? Or was the chattering because of what had happened, and his spirit remained inside her, but such an event would naturally be followed by the deepest chills? But there was no asking anyone on earth, for we haven't been created to know it.

She lay beside him, holding him, her arm over his chest, her body pressed up against the side of his now still and lifeless body, which had been breathing mere moments before, and she knew that her brain was a small and useless, earthbound thing that would never understand, and that she would never be able to properly reconstruct what she had just experienced.

Later, walking in the garden out behind his house, another hour deep into the middle of the night, she knew that the universe had ejaculated his spirit into her – and was it still in her? What if, when she was shivering and chilled and her teeth were chattering, half an hour after it happened, it was because his spirit had suddenly left her? She will never know, and there is no authority on earth who can say what happened that night. It was happening on the spiritual plane – it was not a physical, psychological, or emotional phenomenon, so she will never understand.

When the doctor came later that night to proclaim him dead, and took her hand and said, *Sorry for your loss*, standing there with this new, joyful and loving spirit inside of her, she almost laughed at this strange word he was using, *loss*.

When Mira thinks about her father's death, or the few days of his dying, certain elements are returned to her: his bedroom, the smell of his body from under the sheets as he moved his legs and the air escaped, and she smelled a sort of shit she had never before smelled, intensely pungent, a shit that was also tar. She remembers the darkness of his room, a room which she had known: the bookshelves, the desk beside the bed, and the chair beside the bed that she sometimes sat in that week. How her uncle had put up cardboard-backed prints of paintings, leaning them against the windows to block out the light, and a green towel which he had taped up. From where did he get the tape? She remembers the pink towel on the floor by her father's bed, where he placed his feet, and the bathroom rug she had brought and eventually put in place of the towel; it was fluffier, warmer, and it didn't slip. Her uncle thought he would not appreciate the change, but he did. No, the towel on the floor wasn't pink. It was green. Colours matter. Colours can be hard to remember.

There was the smell of the beeswax candle that she ordered online, which burned the entire time on the little white-and-black-flecked plate. There was the deep yellow of the candle. There was the pink glass of the scented lamp which she had brought from home with its scent of fresh linen, which became too strong to keep burning. Those scents were the scent of the room, mixed with the smell of her father dying, and the difficult sound of his breathing, which she missed each time she left the room. It was like the sound of the sea, or a boat on the sea; aching, creaking, rhythmic, hard. It was difficult for him to breathe, but she loved the sound, and the sound also pained her and put her in a trance. Whenever she went downstairs, if she was gone for too long, she longed for it. It was the sound of him alive, and the very last sounds he made. Though the last sound he made was no sound at all – the sound of the breath that did not come.

The more she thinks about the sort of maroonish light in his room those nights, and the light of the candle flickering, she knows that the colour of that room is how they all felt, and that colour is not just a representation of the world, but of the feelings in a room, and the meaningfulness of a room in time, because in that colour, her father died. She had never seen that colour before. It was the colour of a father dying.

In the days before her father died, she felt all her memories of him disappearing; everything he ever said was gone. She thought, *Oh, life is so stupid, it all means nothing, nothing we do ever lasts, what is the point of it all?*

On those final days, with him mostly unconscious, and sometimes a bit conscious, and sometimes squeezing her hand, she felt how precious it was to be in a room with him, and she wished she had done it more, just gone over to his house with no expectation of talking, just sitting in a room. She suddenly understood how much he had needed that, and now she understood its value, and how lonely it would have been for him not to have had it enough, and now it was all she wanted too, and they would never have it again.

Control your mind, she told herself sternly and seriously through his final hours and days. She knew his death was sending her into the future, and she wanted it to be a bearable one. *Control your mind*, she said to herself, so she wouldn't go down the deepest path of recrimination and despair. What were the words that came into her mind, as she lay with him in the darkness of his final days? *For there is nothing either good or bad, but thinking makes it so.*

It seemed to her the week her father was dying that nothing mattered but art and literature. That while people passed away, the soul of a great artist would stay; that what they made would never die, so they were the ones we could hold close forever. Art would never leave us like a father dying. In a way, it would always remain. Artists manifested themselves in art, not the world, so humans could encounter them there, forever. People could return to books at any time and find them right there, those burning souls, their words as bright as the day they were written. How Mira loved artists! How she loved books, as she lay in bed with her dying father. She saw how great art was, as she lay in his bed, and how faithful; how faithful a book was, and how strong, a place you could be safe, apart from the world, held inside a world that would never grow weak, and which could pass through wars, massacres and floods – could pass through all of human history, and the integrity of its soul would stay strong. A writer could suspend their soul in language, making the souls of writers like droplets of oil, suspended in the sea of life. You couldn't see the water, but you could see the drops, clear little circles, buoyant and complete. To be in a world in which the writers she loved had once lived and written beautifully – that meant there was something real to find here. Art had mattered to her most of all, but her father mattered, also, yet now she saw why she hadn't been the daughter he'd wanted her to be; because art had meant more to her than any human being, it meant more to her than her father did. Her love for her father was great, but her love for books was greater. Had he known this? He once called her selfish. She knew that she had loved her father more than many other people loved theirs. But there was something she loved above her father. This was something they had never seen or could even understand. She didn't even see it until he lay there, dying. Then, in bed with him, her arm across his rising chest, rising and falling those remaining days, and staring at his bookshelf, at all six volumes of Churchill's memoirs, she realised this bottom truth about the nature of her love, and that there was no bottom below this bottom.

His spirit was sly as a fox, the way it snuck into her – the way it stealthily, like a fox, moved into her. She can still feel it there, sometimes, sneaking about. It is a great joy to have his spirit inside her, like the brightest and youngest fox! It rests when it wants to, it moves when it wants to, it lives out its days, in her. So many gifts her father gave her, so she should not be surprised they continued to be given, even in the moment of his dying. His whole life had been a giving to her of his life, and even in death he was giving; like in a fable when a poor man pulls a handful of jewels, emeralds and sapphires from an empty linen sack. So it was as if pulled from his dead body – that empty sack – were the brightest and most shimmering stars, which were his entire spirit.

She had held him when he died, and the heat that filled her was his spirit entering, which spread through the interior of her innermost darkness with an exploding and infinite light.

But she doesn't know the rules of the spirit world, so she will never be able to explain.

In the weeks that followed her father's dying, her mind returned and returned her to it, but she could no more re-create what happened than she could physically return to the past. It was impossible to properly recall it, meaning that she would only know if his spirit had entered her if she had been changed.

But how does she know if she has been changed, or if she just so much wants to be changed that since it happened, she has been pretending?

Yet now she feels exactly how she always wanted to feel, like all her deficiencies have been filled up, all her sorry spaces, and all her spiritual empties. Her sufferings, her stupidities, her utter inabilities, which no instructions or reminders to herself and no aging or learning could ever correct – her father's spirit filled up these empty spaces like water filling up a half-empty cup, or an entire table of half-empty cups. Why? It was perhaps one of two things: the last gift her father, in his generosity, gave her, or else this is what the universe always intended to happen, to complete and make whole the life within her with the addition of her father's spirit, bearing all the gifts and wisdom that her own self was lacking.

The gifts of patience, perspective and detachment.

The gifts of silence, irrelevance and joy.

The day or second day after he died, she saw falling from the sky the first sprinklings of snow. She had never felt a greater quiet in her mind or soul. She cared nothing for the world's busy activity. She felt in competition with no one. ■

Claire Schwartz

Letter by Letter

In his office in the attic, in his favorite khaki pants,
the Archivist carefully sets down the glass case
of his body so as not to rattle the exhibit of his mind.
He wears gloves to stroke the name on the envelope,
the name written in a florid hand trained by long-ago
love. *To live among the dead*, the Archivist thinks.
His eyebrows do a little jig. With fingers strange
to his wife, the Archivist traces the name of the street
in the village that burned. The street wears the name of the flower
the Archivist's mother tucked behind her ear in a photograph
languishing in a desk drawer. The Archivist carries his mind
into each house. Here, the Cook makes love, his hand
brushing flour against his boyfriend's nipple. There,
the Tailor's satisfied song of scissors bisecting
a ream of red. A girl whose mouth makes an O
around which chocolate makes another mouth runs
through the road. The road which runs through
the Archivist's blood. The girl is the Archivist's grandmother
in that she is a story the Archivist tells
himself about how he got here. Under an oak tree,
two dogs fucking. The girl's ice cream is melting.
The Archivist's mind is sticky with history.
Of course, the village burns again. History is
the only road that survives. Downstairs, the Archivist's daughter
is hungry. He restores the dead to their folders. *To live!*
The girls' wails rise through the house like smoke.

CAROL M. HIGHSMITH
Hall of Mirrors at Ripley's Believe It or Not!, Grand Prairie, Texas, USA, 2014
Courtesy of the Library of Congress

IN THE HEART OF THE
HALL OF MIRRORS

Chris Dennis

I was seventeen when I moved to Enfield, Illinois, a village with a population of 600, to live with my mother. I had only seen her twice over the past few years. At fourteen I ran away from home to live with a man who was nearly a decade older than me. My parents were divorced, and before my mother moved to Enfield, she and my father had been living in separate apartments on opposite sides of the Saline County Housing Projects. My mother had a new boyfriend then, who had pinned me to the wall by my throat because I'd said I didn't think the Bible was divinely inspired. He was one of those guys who'd sober up every few months and become very emotional about Christianity. When I left home they all thought I was living with the other parent. When they found out where I was, they were either too uncomfortable to say anything or too consumed by their own tragedies to make me come home.

My boyfriend was a horny, depressed 24-year-old who worked as a paramedic. He liked horror movies and comic books and was occasionally suicidal. The first time he threatened to kill himself was after I'd mentioned wanting to go to a concert with a friend. He liked for me to sit at work with him, watching TV on a busted sofa during the long hours between emergency calls. One time I rode along in the ambulance with him while he transported a body to a medical examiner in Indiana. Over the course of a few years he groomed me, perhaps unintentionally, to depend only on him, to distrust my parents and to always be afraid of losing him. Our last summer together a friend came by to ask if I would spend the weekend with her. He smiled from his favorite chair as she stood in our living room, and rolled us two joints to take, but when he called her house the next day and we weren't there, he left several increasingly desperate messages on her mother's answering machine, threatening that if I didn't come home, I'd never see him again. When my friend finally brought me back early Sunday morning, I was vibrating with panic and guilt. There were three kitchen knives laid out neatly on the coffee table, and a dramatic trail of pills leading to the kitchen sink. He wasn't home. I insisted she leave me there to wait.

Maybe the thing with scaring children is that it'll keep them close for a while – really close – but eventually they'll be too afraid to stay. We fought when he came home, and a week later I left to move back in with my mother.

Until I was almost thirty, I'd have probably told you I loved my adult boyfriend and that he was fun and bought me things and that I felt desired and cared for by him, and that the only thought I had when he first grabbed me in a friend's dark kitchen to kiss me was, 'Holy shit this guy is so hot.' But not long after my own son became a teenager, I started to feel very different about fourteen-year-old Chris's relationship with this grown man. I began to rethink the very nature of adolescence. My child – this more competent, braver reflection of me, who looks so much like me that people have mistaken us for one another at a distance, but who is not me at all – has been guided by his mother with such insistent, nurturing force. She has instilled in him a sense of personal responsibility and self-management that I didn't have access to at his age.

Once when my son was four or five and still slept next to me every night I dreamt that I was having a conversation with a photograph of my grandfather that sat on the dresser in my bedroom. He said to me, 'Someone is walking up the stairs in your apartment.' And I could hear that they were. I was asleep and we lived alone but I could hear the sound of footsteps ascending the stairs, walking into the bedroom, right up to the bed. I felt a hand on my back, someone very gently placing their entire wide-open palm right between my shoulders, and I opened my eyes. My son, who was facing me in the bed, opened his eyes too, so that we were staring directly at each other. He looked at me, then his gaze traveled to something right behind me and a look of terror crept over his small child-face. He said, angrily, 'Who is behind you?'

'Why are you saying that?' I answered, louder and more accusatory than I meant to sound. But then he just closed his eyes again and fell asleep. I sat up and turned around. No one was there. It was just us alone in the room.

How does one relate to a child, except to walk back down that sad sidewalk on the way home from school, on a dry fall day, past the convenience store where my mother worked the second shift, toward the apartment where we lived, to meet a grown man who was waiting in his car on a side street to pick me up and drive me to a cornfield or a wooded area where we would – my God in fucking hell what was I doing out there all alone in the world?

It hurts to think of my mother reading this now. I do not want her to feel some grief over the past, because even if she'd tried to stop me from running away with the man, some bit of damage had already been done long before, and I still would have gone. I'd been heading toward him, or someone like him, for years.

This might be one of the kinder mirrors parenthood will hold up to your terrified, startled face: your own treacherous youth, offering a grain of empathy to build a full-grown fatherly heartache around. It's an ugly road back to these moments where you now have to reparent yourself, knowing you're the only one who understands enough about it to do the job right, with your newfound powers of consideration, and a new ability to comfort yourself.

*

My mother – such a tiny lady but with very long hair, like a wig. If it falls across her face while she is driving with the windows down, she will adjust it, carefully, with just her fingernail. She still carries a vast, shape-shifting version of religion, one that demands at times a tormented judgment of herself and others. She smiles so easily at little children. I have seen her be both generous and darkly critical in her assumptions about others' intentions. Of course you already know this. Likely I've told you before. I've told you all of this. But I'm going to tell you again. My mother and I share a tendency to grow tired around people, even when it's someone we adore, but are sometimes overwhelmed with affection toward them later when we're alone, eating chips on the porch after dark. We are better at reflecting than reacting. We are very good at sitting in uncertainty. Or maybe we're not. We like giving gifts – personal, expertly crafted gifts that prove what good listeners we are. Or maybe we never actually give them. Daydreaming is one way of planning the friendships we long to have. Our intentions must seep out just enough. Because I have found friends. I have found such astounding friends.

In a recent letter to my friend Gina I explained how I'd been thinking about the Carl Jung quote, 'The greatest burden a child must bear is the unlived life of its parents.' I explained how the quote unsettled me, because I worry my son has witnessed his father in too many pitiful moments, watched me made into a wretched person – addicted and incarcerated and unable to cope with the regular strain of a heavy life. But then I think of all the times he has seen me with my friends, when I'm good, when I'm most alive, when I'm seized by messy laughter at some depraved thing. I love that he's sat on porch steps with my friends and me, watching us cackle at our own sideways jokes. It makes me feel at home in my own body. I like that my son has seen his father turn to comedy as a means of self-criticism, that he's seen the sharp knife of my friends' wit cut through his father's own bad ideas, that he's watched our attempts to dismantle the terrible things around us by making fun of them.

Some of the best memories of my mother are of her laughing at an old, horrible mistake, seeing her come undone with her friends when she is not my mother, or she is some new mother who cracks open her discomfort with humor. I remember one of her oldest friends swinging open our back door in the middle of the day, saying, 'Some guy just drove through the alley behind my house with his dick out!' My mother drew back in disgust, 'What did you say to him?' Her friend shrugged, and threw her hands out, 'I told him to come back later.' My mother's face froze. She looked at me, then back at her friend, before letting out a laugh so piercing and sincere that it scared me.

Sometimes when I talk about my mother and father, my friend Amy will paraphrase the French psychoanalyst Jacques Lacan, saying, 'Every child is the miscarriage of their parents' unattainable desires.' Does it not chill your bones? It is difficult not to conjure a gruesome, improbable image.

While I was incarcerated Amy sent me the collected works of Oscar Wilde. She wanted me to read *De Profundis* ('From the Depths'), a long letter that Wilde wrote from prison in Reading. 'You should make notes or highlight things, so we can talk about it over the phone,' she said. Phone calls from jail are timed, and expensive, so it helped to plan things out. Here are some of the things I underlined while reading on my bunk: 'A sentimentalist is simply one who desires to have the luxury of an emotion without paying for it.' And, 'At every single moment of one's life one is what one is going to be no less than what one has been. Art is a symbol, because man is a symbol.'

Wilde remembers his awful trial. The prosecution attempted to illustrate his perversities, to criminalize evidence of his desire for other men. Some of his friends were called as witnesses, even a few men he'd once flirted with at a party. What would my friends say if they were called to explain every hookup and weird desire I've confided in them? Would you say, 'Oh, Chris? So sane. So very, very sane.' Because our love is a secret palace?

Wilde writes about how sickened he was by the horrors he heard, until suddenly it occurred to him in prison: 'How splendid it would be, if I was saying all this about myself. I saw then at once that what is said of a man is nothing. The point is, who says it.'

So much of the anxiety that swallowed me up every day in jail was the fear of what my friends were thinking. You have to pay for the privilege to communicate with the outside world, and so I would have to wait weeks and months for the chance to explain all of my mistakes to them myself.

Time has a way of turning us against or toward ourselves. Laughing is also a way of controlling the narrative of our own failures, of strangling darkness with parody. It grants me a sense of authority over my life, in the simplest terms, a sense that I am the author of it, even if it only means carrying the world one piece at a time into the mirror-filled halls of my imagination.

That empty summer before my eighteenth birthday when I moved back in with my mother she'd only been living in Enfield for a few months, staying in the house of my great-grandmother, who had moved into a nursing home a few streets over. It was fifteen miles of vacant highway to the nearest restaurant or store. As far as I knew I was the only teenager in town, and I had no car. Until then my mother had never really had a home to herself. Her boyfriend had moved out, and later died in a drunk-driving accident. I returned to find her a single woman for the first time in her adult life.

There was an extra bedroom, with the palest green walls, where I would hide and smoke pot and listen to Fleetwood Mac and meticulously cut and paste little pictures from *Spin* magazine until I'd covered nearly half the room. I'd already dropped out of high school. I watched out the window each morning as my mother walked over to the neighbor's to sit on the porch with her new friend, Joanne. Joanne was originally from Boston, and almost seventy. She was wonderfully loud, her voice hanging in her throat. She had large plastic eyeglasses and a uniform cloud of gray hair teased around her chalky face. She was a fan of polyblend slacks, and long earrings. She would scream across the yard at my window every day for me to come over and sit on the porch, 'Christopher! Christopher, come over and talk to your mother and I! You're not going to sit indoors.' For Joanne, the real moments of a person's life only occurred outdoors. And so of course I did, and without really meaning to or knowing it was happening Joanne became my friend too, because she was my mother's friend and because her laugh was so shrill and filled up her small body so thoroughly. She loved to talk about herself, and told me violent stories of organized crime during her childhood in the city. This was thrilling to someone who'd only ever seen the small towns of southern Illinois. I loved her old life, which was the point, to have my mother and me fall in love with her life and then, in turn, with her. She had an intense collection of antique candy dishes and several paintings of the Virgin Mary purchased from mail-order catalogues and would sometimes, if the conversation dragged, bring us inside to show them to us. Joanne kept a small garden and would call us over to pick tomatoes for her while she sat on the porch yelling, 'No!' if we reached for one she didn't think was ripe. Perhaps my mother was lonely, because Joanne wasn't always kind, or maybe my mother found some sort of strength in being helpful to someone for whom gratitude didn't come easy. Maybe a constant longing for ungiven thanks was something my mother had grown used to. It was instructive, though, to watch her being a good friend to someone she only barely knew.

If the heart has a great hall then it must also have a dungeon. There are obviously mirrors on the ceiling of the dungeon of one's life, too. We may review the little tortures as if they're happening to someone else. From one angle this offers perspective, from another it allows us to behave like a judgmental voyeur, even to ourselves. I have a learned tendency to criticize my own capacity for pain, even if I'm the one inflicting it. This is one of the mirror's greatest tricks, to display another you that you can blame for the very things you have done to yourself.

What I mean to say is, I have learned from my friends how crucial it can be to tilt your head a bit if you're feeling bad, as a way of checking to see if it's you or the world who's behaving badly.

I stayed with my mother in my great-grandmother's house for a year, and in the summer of 1999 Joanne died of lung cancer. It was a smoldering-hot day and I walked the three blocks down the main street in Enfield to the only funeral parlor in town. I stood there sweating quietly beneath the drop ceilings, staring at the dated decor, the uninspired landscape paintings and fake flowers. I was in an ugly pair of pants and a shirt I'd bought the day before at a thrift store in Carmi, not really knowing anyone except my mother, who was talking with the other neighbors. There is no way to say this correctly, to convey the terror, but I had forgotten that Joanne had an identical twin. Surely I had met her once? But when her sister came walking into the funeral parlor my body felt stunned along every nerve ending, and I was instantly someone who did not know himself, or where he was. It was not a matter of ghosts or the undead, but instead an absolute distrust in reality. I thought, 'Oh, wait – I'm not at a funeral. I'm at a party. Who invited me here?' I could only imagine that I had misunderstood the event. Why did I even think I was at a funeral?

When I told you this story, twenty years later, Melissa – because it has suddenly become very clear to me that all along this was a letter to you – you laughed. And the joke was: what a fantastic crack in reality! Isn't it good to be known in this way? We grew up in the same county, but didn't know each other until we were just old enough to drink. We share a delirious joy in the hysterias of childhood, in the charming stupidity of adolescence, and a certainty that at any given moment reality is a bold, ridiculous fucking lie. Even if we can't always make it out or point directly at it, we know the change in perspective is coming; any second, the mirrors will shift and there will be a better version of the world beneath or above or beside the one we're experiencing now. It's comforting of course to know that pain will change. We might only be standing a little further back, but from here, it's hysterical.

Isn't it reassuring how naturally our children reflect this allegiance to the kingdom of the absurd? Isn't it something to see their brilliant disregard of principles, that my mostly reserved, straight son indulges our acidic queer theatrics, that he's seen the trashiest parts of life refined in the campiest fires of his father's faggot heart? Would it be too much for me to mention now how many generations of descendants it took to complete the Palace of Versailles? Every numbered Louis seemed more unhinged than the last, all of them taking their turn, standing inside the original Hall of Mirrors. By then the royal home was a maze of grandiose camp. It took multiple lifetimes for it to arrive there. Isn't it funny to think about, looking back on our own little lives spent in so many trailer parks, and at all the times our parents turned on the utilities in our names to avoid paying the previous bill? Somehow, against their first impulse for us to be nurses or gas station managers, we became writers. Ha ha ha ha ha ha. How did that happen? Or does it make perfect sense? 'Art is a symbol, because man is a symbol.'

A friendship can be a terrifying, marvelous risk, an attempt to rise out of your own body and into someone else's, because a friend is also sometimes a way of discovering another self, a surprise twin in the funeral parlor of life.

Perhaps what I also mean to say, Melissa, is that during those hateful months I spent in jail I had a dream that I was sitting at one end of a very lengthy antique dining table and you were seated at the opposite end. The table was spread with an enormous amount of vivid, polished wax fruit – even in my dreams the metaphors are food-related – and we were laughing raucously, to the point of tears, because we were both so very hungry and had sat down to enjoy a beautiful feast when we realized that all the food was fake. We were ravenous. And somehow that was the funny part. It's as if we both understood that if all there was to consume was comedy, that warped variety of joy, we would fill ourselves up until there was room for nothing else. ■

To catch an octopus needs stillness. And a keen pair of eyes.

Nothing more, nothing less.

August or September is best for then the young ones are alone, their mothers gone back to the deep and left them in more shallow water altogether. Pick a gorge that casts shadows between flat-sided cliffs, each side cratered enough to easily climb. If the pool at the bottom is deep but no wider than a well, so much the better: such a space will be calm even when the rest is wild. Check the speed of the incoming tide; note whether the water is rising or ebbing away. You do not want to drown. Note the pits in the cliff, their patterns and places so that when you descend, you will have hand- and footholds enough to be secure. A great many pits are a good thing: below the surface, they make hiding places for fish and molluscs and boneless little bodies. Then, the route sure, begin. Keeping your face to the rock, your fingers taut, slip over the edge. Dig your toes into each foothold to test for slime or settled occupants before trusting your weight: test handholds the same. Something with claws will fight back. In this way, descend till your heels meet the water and the light above has grown less bright. Listen for the current. A lap like a cat means gentle. Steady your cheek against the rock and look down. Check what depth is visible. Hope there is sand beneath, not broken pottery or razor shells. And when you are sure, breathe deep and drop.

Drop. The shock is momentary.

Open your eyes.

Observe shapes made by light as the waves shift, all that may be movement. They know already you are there. Ignore the starfish. Ignore the crabs. What is not languid is not your concern. Let your arms be weightless, your shoulders drop, and wait. Wait. And they will come. Like phantoms from secret spaces, of their own accord, they will come despite themselves for they are curious, unable to resist. One at first, small as a fist, her little arms unfurling to find your wrist, encircle it with kidskin. She may trace your open palm. It is her nature to explore. Now she is caught by curiosity, your test is this: do nothing. Let her tender her embrace and grow easy. Slowly, touch back. And she will curl with pleasure, press against your hand like a kitten, wanting more. When she is grown, her beak will slice to the bone for then she knows you are treacherous, but for now, she is a child. She has no guile. Let St Francis be your guide. A wild thing has found you. In that you are blessed. Let her stay until your lungs demand the surface, your own element. One day she will populate whole seas. Let her stay here. Do no harm. Spread your fingers. Watch her flex. Turn your face to the light as she goes

she goes

she goes

LEWIS KHAN
from *Theatre*

WAITING ROOM

Will Rees

Some time ago while riding the Tube, I came across an advertisement that stood out among the familiar roster of ads for nutritional supplements and blended Tennessee whiskey. This was in the days before the pandemic emptied Tube carriages and transformed indoor public spaces into chambers of contagion. Unfolding across several posters, it went like this: 'Explore risks that may be common in your family tree.' 'See how DNA affects your health.' 'Put your worries to test.'

The advertisement was clearly suggesting that the knowledge it sold would be beneficial to the customer, although why and in what ways were questions on which it demurred with an undergraduate essayist's dictional prudence: not 'mitigate' or 'minimise' but *explore risks*. The claim seemed to be that knowing about one's genetic predispositions to disease would be inherently good. Knowledge itself would be improving.

Yes, I thought. I could see myself doing that, in the spirit of exploration.

A few years earlier, my aunt died. It was very sudden, no one saw it coming. She was young – about forty – and not manifestly in ill health. One evening she went to bed, and the following morning she was carried downstairs.

In the desultory, strange days that followed, we were told by the pathologist that she had suffered a cerebral event – an aneurysm or a stroke. Afterwards, this was corrected. No, it had in fact been her heart that malfunctioned.

For years afterwards I could never remember whether it was my aunt's brain or her heart which was defective, and even now I am uncertain. I only remember that there was some initial confusion, now long since resolved, but which is the correct explanation and which the false I continue to forget. I've asked my mother countless times to clarify matters, but – and not for any lack of interest on my part or clarity on hers – I do not seem capable of retaining the knowledge. My ignorance on the matter persists in spite, or perhaps because, of the possibility of a genetic link.

Throughout my early twenties I spent a lot of time seeking to acquire knowledge about my body. It was unwell, this much was certain, and the question of how was one to which I applied myself studiously. Of course, I had theories. Looking back, these tended to change quite frequently. My researches required me to enlist the help of doctors. Above all, I sought a scan that would light up every region of my body; that would reveal, clearly and distinctly, what was the matter with it. It is a long story; it went on for some time. Then something happened.

One evening I fell sick. I had a fever, I didn't sleep. Nevertheless, the following morning I felt fine, and went to work. But that evening the fever came back, this time worse. This cycle continued for a week or two.

At the time, I was an outreach worker. This was in 2012, or possibly 2013, the early days of austerity. It was January. The work involved traipsing the streets of north London to inform its elderly inhabitants of which services remained. I was working under the aegis of a new charity whose main funders were the councils in which it operated (in many ways it was, I'd later come to understand, a roundabout and insidious form of privatisation). I was paid handsomely for this work, but by the hour. What was more, it was seasonal; once temperatures reached double digits, this brief and surprisingly lucrative employment would cease.

I quickly adapted my routine to these new realities. I'd get up, without having slept, and put my bed sheets in the washing machine (time delay: seven hours). Then I'd cycle across the river. I'd walk around the council estates of north London, which were now mostly privatised, and knock on some doors. Then I'd cycle back to Camberwell, move my bed sheets from the washing machine to the dryer, eat dinner, wash up, read something and reinstall the freshly laundered sheets. Then I'd fix myself a drink and sit in bed and wait until, just after 11 p.m. and always before 11.20, the fever began to gather. This proved to be surprisingly sustainable, until one day I collapsed on the stairs.

I took a morning off work to visit my GP. It was an expensive visit from the perspective of earnings potential. As usual, Dr C was patrician and inscrutable. His body had been trained over many years to be semantically neutral, to give nothing away. He nodded as I explained what had happened, and then, as if dismissing everything I'd just said, he said, 'OK, let's have a look at you.' He placed a stethoscope on my back in order to listen to my lungs, placing his other hand against my chest to steady himself. His grip tightened, signifying something. He cleared his throat and composed himself. 'Did you have any plans today, Mr Rees?'

Dr C instructed me to go to A & E. They would X-ray me today; it would have to be today. I agreed to go straight there. After I left his office, Dr C followed me out into the stairwell and called out, 'You will go straight there, won't you, Mr Rees?'

At the hospital I explained all this to the triage nurse. I was careful to leave nothing out, but also to make no embellishments. She nodded sympathetically and drank in every detail: his tightening grip, the atmosphere that hung about the room. His haunted tone as he called out to me across the waiting room. When my narrative was over she handed me a piece of paper and asked me to hand it in at reception. The paper read: 'Feels unwell.'

Later that day I had an X-ray. True enough, there was a 'mass' in my lungs. Certainly, it was of some concern. But it was impossible to say what the mass was ('an X-ray machine is not a precise instrument, young man'). A long period of waiting followed, interrupted by the women who occasionally appeared to take samples of my blood. I regretted having brought nothing to read.

For many hours I sat there, bookless and bored, until eventually a junior doctor appeared to tell me how things stood. The results that had come back were normal. Others would take longer. It was possible that I had a virus of some sort. That would explain the chest X-ray: it would be a lymph node, that was all. On the other hand, there were reasons to doubt it. My white cell count was normal. One would expect it to be raised. Things did suggest that something more sinister might be going on, but it was too soon to be jumping to conclusions. I wasn't to worry. I was to go now, get some rest. I was to come back tomorrow, when I would report to the Medical Assessment Centre.

Honestly, this was not unwelcome. In general, the parameters of any medical investigation are determined by the story that one tells about oneself. When one leaves a doctor's office having been told, after a brief examination, not to worry, that what one had taken to be a concerning symptom is merely one of the ordinary vexations of embodiment – that one is, in a word, healthy – the feeling tends to be reassuring only in the short term. Before long, doubts set in. What if one has failed to give the really essential piece of information? What if the small detail which in the blur of the encounter slipped one's mind, or which, in embarrassment at one's paratactic excesses, one deliberately withheld, what if this detail were the truly important thing, the stray thread which would have enabled the doctor to unweave the veil of health and reveal the sick body beneath?

Such, at least, tended to be my experience. In *King Lear* Cordelia laments, 'I cannot heave my heart into my mouth.' She is referring to her inability to give voice to interiority, to perform a private feeling of love. A patient must heave their entire body into their mouth.

They must rally the forces of intellect in order to give an account of a body whose nature is independent of their ability to account for it in language but whose fate now depends on that ability. There is always more one can say, and if the patient fails to say the correct thing then any reassuring words uttered by the doctor will be worse than null; they will be a lure. And yet giving a good account of oneself, an account which will convince a doctor that one is worthy of their time, a reliable witness to one's own body, is also about knowing what not to say. More really isn't always more. It is a writer's problem: what to put in, leave out. But the stakes are different.

The Medical Assessment Centre promised deliverance from the usual cycle of relief and regret. It promised that medicine's investigations into my body would no longer depend upon my skill as a narrator. At the Medical Assessment Centre I would be reduced to a mute object of medical knowledge, anonymous and transparent like an anatomical drawing. The thought delighted me.

When I arrived the next morning at the Medical Assessment Centre, the receptionist, whom I had never met, knew my name. Actually, everyone there seemed to know me. Over the course of that morning people of various professions made reference to my 'case'.

I changed into a hospital gown. A nurse came to take some blood and, to my surprise, left a cannula in my arm. 'Oh?' I said. 'Don't worry, Mr Rees,' she said meaningfully. 'For your procedure.' A few minutes later a hospital porter arrived with a wheelchair. 'All right, Mr Rees, hop in.' It dawned on me that I might actually be a patient. It was an unlovely realisation that felt nothing at all like vindication. I declined, politely I believe, and said I was perfectly well enough to walk. The porter appeared hurt. He mumbled that he would have to check with the doctor. I nodded that he should do whatever he felt necessary as I gathered my belongings into my rucksack.

The porter returned, bearing no evident resentment, and as we made the short walk to the Imaging Unit he prattled cheerfully about this and that, the weather, his two young children, the extension he was building at his parents' house. When we arrived, he withdrew quickly so that my delayed and oddly inflected 'Goodbye' was addressed to his back as he receded through the double doors.

At the IU, I was injected with a coloured dye that made my asshole dilate and passed several times through a noisy, large machine. It was the moment I'd been waiting for, my dream come true. Afterwards I was told (without the offer of a wheelchair) to retrace my steps to the Medical Assessment Centre. I sat around for an hour or two, time now completely lost to me, although its passing was tortuous, until the kindly, brusque Dr L appeared. 'Look, it's going to be a while. Go for a walk, get something to eat. OK?'

Dr L said he'd call me as soon as he had the results. Soon I was sitting in a dimly lit coffee shop holding a book, and after an hour, or some hours, I received the call from Dr L. His voice now sounded completely different, grave, formal, although it was difficult to know what to make of this since he belonged to a class and a generation whose members still possessed a 'phone voice'.

I sensed that my fate was now known – not yet to me, but to someone. The facts of the matter had come to light; it only remained for them to be conveyed to me. As I stepped out into the street I had a sudden rush of appreciation for ignorance, which I now realised could be something more than a mere deficit. Ignorance could have a reality of its own, it could be a state of plenitude and possibility. It was a state in which I'd have liked to abide a little longer, perhaps indefinitely.

The sky was luminous and white. It was one of those overcast days that give one the appalling sensation of living inside a fluorescent light bulb. I thought about walking in the opposite direction to the hospital, to the Thames, perhaps, or to the City, where I rarely ventured, but whose shadowy and impersonal labyrinth of skyscrapers seemed to offer the very opposite of what lay in store for me at the Medical Assessment Centre. I thought about never returning, taking my chances.

Of course, I walked straight to the hospital. It wasn't only that a will to knowledge turned out to be the stronger drive. The pleasures of not knowing are necessarily belated. One can always choose not to know. But ignorance, consciously chosen, is nothing at all like innocence.

When I returned, Dr L greeted me at the door. He told me to follow him into a private room, his voice still grave. I sat on the bed, he on the lid of a metal bin marked BIOWASTE. On the computer screen were the results of a CT scan: my body, illuminated. I was surprised to find myself not feeling very anxious. It was not a feeling of calm that came over me, however; only abandonment to the implacable logic of the situation.

Dr L was going to cut to the chase. The scan showed what he had hoped it would not show, that all through my body my lymph nodes were enlarged. They were, in Dr L's phrase, 'standing to attention', although he could not say why. What he was saying was, the image was clear enough. But he could not explain what it meant.

A disease was mentioned whose name had long been prominent in my daydreams and internet browsing history. Hearing its name said aloud (I think for the first time), this felt obscene and electrifying. Infection was mentioned too, although it was with a tone of regret that Dr L reiterated that there was no elevation in my white cell count. It was of some concern that the enlarged nodes were distributed evenly above and beneath my diaphragm. 'That will make it late stage,' I offered. 'The ones that concern me are in your chest,' he said. 'They're very deep.'

That I liked Dr L was partly because he always spoke as though enlisting your assistance to some shared task. He started every sentence with an imperative, 'Look', and ended it with a rhetorical, 'OK?'. These were obvious affectations, which did not make them less effective; his style made any response feel weirdly pedantic, and in an infantilised desire to prove myself to Dr L by matching his aloofness I could almost forget that the item under discussion was my own body.

'Look, nothing is certain yet. There's still a chance that this is just an infection. In which case, in a couple of weeks you're going to forget all about it. Get on with your life. But in the meantime, we're going to have to do a lot more tests. OK?' I nodded. 'Look, I know all this is frightening. But I can promise that we're going to get to the bottom of this. So, come back here tomorrow at nine and we'll get started, OK?' I nodded.

What followed was a fortnight during which I reported each morning to the Medical Assessment Centre. Sometimes I spent an entire day there, other times it was only a fleeting visit to deposit a little blood en route to north London, whose elderly population awaited news about what would survive the cutbacks to public expenditure that were reported to be 'swingeing' (one of those words that, everywhere for a short time, one rarely hears afterwards).

Many tests were performed, and aside from ordinary pleasantries I was rarely required to speak. I simply handed myself over. That the fever had gone by this time was not considered a reason to desist; now, and for the very first time, medicine had taken an interest in my body that had nothing to do with my experience of it.

One day I had a fine-needle biopsy to determine whether the cells that had clumped into masses inside my right armpit were cancerous; it would take a week or more for the results to come back. The intervening period was colourless and strange, and the waiting rooms in which I often sat came to seem like a metaphor for life itself.

On the other hand, I was learning a lot. Partly by osmosis – I was spending so much time on the ward – and partly because of the hospital's practice of copying patients in to all correspondence between its consultants and the patient's GP. Due to a time lag of three or four days, these letters would always arrive a little out of sync with where things currently stood. This did not render them an irrelevance, however, since, addressed not to me but to my GP, they presented information about my case in a way that was completely unfamiliar.

The feeling when reading these letters was similar to overhearing a conversation about one's behaviour at a recent party. The deviation from one's own memory need not at all be great for it to kill one on the spot. In these curt yet suggestive letters there would frequently be reference to things that had never been discussed with me ('ACE level elevated'; 'liver function abnormalities'; 'inconclusive') while matters which I'd considered settled days earlier were repeatedly thrown back into question. And so while the letters fizzed with information – information that I would immediately augment with further information drawn from Google searches – I tended to come away from having read them feeling more, not less, in the dark.

In the third volume of the *Spheres* trilogy – a towering philosophical history of the West – the philosopher Peter Sloterdijk argues that modernity is underwritten by 'explication', a process by which previously unthematised background aspects of life are drawn into the foreground. As this occurs, what had passed for simple is revealed in all its previously unimagined complexity: for instance *air*, previously the undifferentiated medium of existence, is shown to be a mixture of gases subject to countless fluctuations. On the one hand this increases our technical mastery over the environment; on the other, it brings a sense of vulnerability. There are so many ways that something complicated can go wrong.

What really interests me about Sloterdijk's argument is this: far from steadily eroding the regions of latency, replacing hazy ignorance with solid facts, explication in fact serves to generate new latencies. As the critic Steven Connor has noted, revelation is always haunted by a feeling of not knowing; as previously unexpected areas of complexity are revealed, thoughts and suspicions loom about what else remains to be brought to light. Where previously there had been nothing at all, now there are depths waiting to be plumbed.

When, after a fortnight or so, it was revealed that I'd had glandular fever – this had initially been ruled out on the basis of an antibody test, but showed up on a subsequent test – I was delighted. It was like one of those criminal judgements in which the accused is given some trivial sentence and, having served this time awaiting trial, is free to go.

The feeling did not last, however. On the day the receptionist told me over the phone about the glandular fever result, I was due to report to the Medical Assessment Centre to get the result of the biopsy. I asked the receptionist if I should still make the appointment, now that we had an explanation. She asked me to hold the line while she discussed this with the consultant – a distant murmuring I could hear but not make out – and when she returned told me, emphatically, that I was indeed required to keep the appointment.

At the appointment, however, which so emphatically was necessary, and which I attended with a frank terror I had not experienced in the two weeks hitherto, the consultant said, after a long preamble about the marvels of the human immune system, that he was confident that the glandular fever result explained the abnormalities he'd found in my biopsy.

'So there were abnormalities in my biopsy?'

'No, no. Well, not once we take into account the glandular fever. I can tell you, I was happy to see that.'

'What about my ACE level?'

'What about it?'

'It's elevated.'

'Oh, it is? Hmm.'

'And my liver function, it's abnormal.'

'Well, in any case it's nothing to worry about. You're *fine*, Mr Rees.' The consultant cheerfully handed me a form discharging me from the care of the Medical Assessment Centre. It was his way of asking me to leave.

I'd been an outpatient of the Medical Assessment Centre for a fortnight, or thereabouts. Now I was leaving, healthy. At home, letters continued to arrive for several days.

The charity I worked for did not give its casualised staff sick pay, and so I did not rest, as was advised. Quite the opposite, since my recent absences had been expensive. Probably the work did me good. My period of employment ended in the spring.

My memories of the period that followed are more clotted, much harder to give an account of besides the vaguest outlines. It is when I came closer than I ever have to madness. Following a brief period of respite, doubts set in. There were so many things which did not make sense. I'd kept much of the correspondence between the hospital and the GP, which, now thumbed and coffee-stained, was full of incongruous details; it seemed to me to provide a lengthy record of leads unpursued.

I started to resemble poor Miss Flite from *Bleak House*, making myself a continual presence at the GP surgery and at the hospital, always, of course, with 'my documents'. There were a good many things that I'd have liked to know, things I would have liked to clear up. A scan, I thought. That would do it. A scan that would light up every region of my body, revealing what was the matter with it. That would require me to enlist the help of doctors. It was a task to which I applied myself vigorously.

It was a dark time, which went on for many months, during which ordinary life, as it is wont, went on too. And then at some point, without ever really concluding, that period of my life ended.

Now, I prefer not to know. I rarely visit doctors; my internet browsing history no longer resembles a diagnostic manual. It has been this way for some years. I don't know how this happened exactly; like any transformation in *Weltanschauung* it had no present tense. It was only possible, afterwards, to observe that I no longer paid any heed to my health. A few years ago I began writing about all this; the fact might be relevant. If I were to become sick now I'd probably be the last to realise. I don't know that this necessarily represents an advance but certainly it has made life pleasanter.

A few weeks ago I noticed a lymph node the size of a conker in my right armpit, and then another. A few days later I visited the doctor, who suggested sending me for an ultrasound. A few days after that, a text message arrived containing a link through which I could book the hospital appointment: the earliest one was four days later, but I could choose from the many available appointments, in various convenient locations, the one that suited me best.

I have not yet booked the appointment, although I have thought of doing so many times. The lymph nodes remain enlarged. I do not feel frightened, but I do continue to put it off. I have been busy, writing. It is only now, in the very final stages of editing this essay, that the thought occurs to me (it is a thought which makes me smile) that these two things – the appointment that I haven't made, and the essay that I have been writing – could be related. ■

Rachel Long

Prom Notes

The velvet rope we would chicken-limbo under
Hey you two, that's VIP!
Girls, girls, girls
our hands clamp
the back of our dresses down
the way our tongues could hold contraband;
gum, a cherry drop,
the morning-after pill
We shimmy under and into –

The white balloon of waiting

boobs about to blow

double lessons swelling

the crush calling

Hello?

Those all-American high-school corridors,
rendered here, in marshiest south-east London.
Waxed blonde pine; new girl limbs
and locker-flanked – not a love note inside.
Not a bad word from a bully either. No
I know what you did last summer
just yesterday's banana
rotting gently in the corner.

And the French-fry sunlight pouring in
through the double doors, the forbidden outside.

Stack the chairs neatly, 9B! I said Neatly!
Leaning tower of lapis. Stacks on stacks on stacks,
bums and laps, lean-back-straddle.

She's holding her breath
because his hand's on her corsaged shoulder

Till uni do us part.

Swear Down/I Promise

I'll remember your full name
and where it came in the register
for the rest of my life.

The straightening
till the irons smoked
and screeched
and the whole top deck
of the 401 sang
of the burning.

The turkey-twizzlering
till the wand smoked
and shrieked
and the hair extensions
slackened
at the almost-root

All that hair
curled and laid
in a line
on the bed
from 5 a.m.

for Vinny
for the kitten
he actually bought her
to be crowned
the hottest girl in year 11.

Bird-shit eyes we called her. So much mascara and white eyeliner!

And the upside-down tiara of her smile.

Baby hairs toothbrushed and laid. Dollar signs.
Nails extra taloned, square-tipped, Tipp-Ex white
Her hand clutching purse, or inna de air.

If you do pink, I'll go red.
One white, one black trainer.
One green eye, one blue
the sharing of all things –
coloured contact lenses, hairbands,
diamanté thongs, phone minutes,
prescriptions, gel pens.
One Barbour, one fake Burberry bag,
one gold dolly necklace
between three best friends.

Prom King, Prom Queen, Prom Kiss, Prom Princess, Prom Jester,
Prom Hater, Prom Prince, Prom Lover, Prom Cruiser, Prom 'Caterer',
Prom Committee, Prom Devotee, Prom Leaver, Prom Dreamer, Prom
Bouncer, Prom Heaver, Prom Shaker, Prom Teaser, Prom Believer

Warren became a mechanic
Delvin prison
Thingy who sat next to Warren had a substance abuse problem
I bumped into Vince and Steve in Canary Wharf once
Only one of them worked there I think.
Did you hear about what happened to Jermaine?
No
Man's a –

History

Miss Grant said I looked like Scarlett O'Hara in my pink ruched satin.
Kyra wore mint. Together we look like a ham sandwich.
That last term I'd written Miss Grant a letter –
what she said about the strange sound probably coming from
Francesca's afro upset me. She was very upset, and then sorry.
It was years till I got around to reading *Gone with the Wind*,
which got me over a very bad break-up.
I carried that book under my arm for weeks, then left it in a pub.
After our prom, Kyra and I realised
we couldn't afford the limo all the way home,
so we asked the driver to catch the night bus up for us.
Here we are, kinda forever, Kyra and I, top deck, a kebab each.

LEAVERS

Lewis Khan

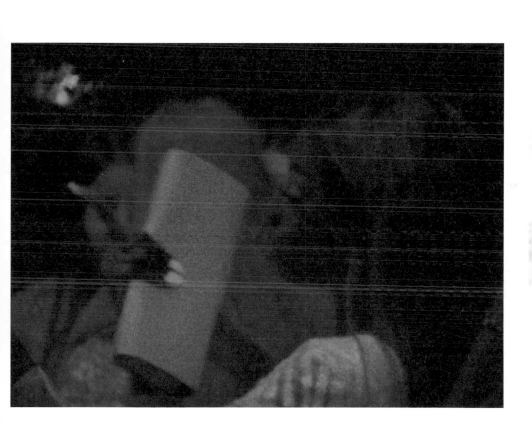

A physician wearing a seventeenth-century plague preventive
Courtesy of the Wellcome Collection

THE PHYSICIAN

Nathan Harris

The physician and the vicar take tea at midday. They speak of the boy who wandered aimlessly through the burgh some months ago, pleading for help, pointing fitfully at the ball of pus weeping beneath his arm. He sought treatment from the physician – for which there was none – and that same evening asked the vicar for the prayers that might heal him. Now, the physician calmly pours the vicar more tea, elaborating on the boy's stench, how it struck him upon examination as the smell of death itself, a manifestation of all that humanity has wrought upon the world, a punishment for a sin so great they might never tease its meaning from the affliction that has now overrun their quiet sliver of a once-great kingdom. The boy is long dead, of course. Buried outside of town in a pile with the rest of the bodies.

The vicar, beside the physician, shifts in his chair, uneasy with the direction of their conversation. 'It is a sorry thing. For relief to be so far beyond our capacities. I did keep him in my prayers. That I did. As I continue to do with the others . . .' The vicar wears gentle colors, a shapeless green habit that belies his station, and his face, wizened and aged, takes on a rustic depiction that matches his clothing (the physician has always appreciated the vicar's features: his drooped eyes, the arched lines that span from his nose to his chin, all of it sloping towards his beard which cuts to a sharp point. His beauty rippling southward like a wave). The vicar goes on. 'These are curious thoughts from someone who has . . . struggled with his faith. It strikes me that they might be born from your loss, Thomas. Is that the case? And you'll excuse me if I speak out of turn. Bringing her up as I have.'

'Rose did not suffer the pestilence,' Thomas tells him bluntly. He does not take offense at the vicar's reach. The man is like an older brother to him, their friendship sparked years ago when the vicar came to his practice in secret, asking for help after sleeping with an unclean woman. They met often after that. Intimate affairs like this one, and although no topic was forbidden, it was not looked down upon to abstain from giving an answer.

'Perhaps we should speak of better things,' the vicar says.

The fireplace sparks with life and spits kindled cedar at the vicar's feet. He makes no mention of it, only smiles, nodding as Thomas sips from his cup.

'How about of Gabriel?' the vicar asks. 'How does he get on?'

'He has only gotten better with patients,' Thomas tells him. 'They are no longer weary of his youth. Of his countenance.'

'One cannot help but appreciate the joy he takes to his work.'

'Not just his *joy*,' Thomas says, quite suddenly finding himself sitting forward on his haunches. 'It is his passion for inquiry. To address not just the pain but to find the source. To truly heal. It is what will make him not just a good physician, but a fine one. Better than myself.'

The windowpane shudders, and as if he had been summoned, Gabriel appears in the doorway, pulling the mask from his face, wiping his hands upon his blouse and letting his cane lean against the side of the door.

He greets them as he walks through the parlor. He then enters the storeroom, the same room where Thomas used to meet his patients. It now houses Gabriel's instruments; collects dust. When Gabriel reemerges, undressed from his costume, Thomas asks after the patient he has treated.

'The blacksmith's son touched a horseshoe before it had cooled,' Gabriel says. 'I believe the father was more upset with his son's lack of knowledge in the family trade than with the injury. A blacksmith apparently does not allow oneself to be burnt. News to the boy.'

Gabriel stands before them, still grinning. His eyes are heavily lidded, as though he is perennially on the verge of sleep. His hair is a messy sweep of black. They have never discussed where it is he hails from. Not the burgh. The people here consider him part mongrel, if only for his looks, and an outsider of such remarkable appearance must operate under the supervision of a man more trustworthy. A man like Thomas. A man, it might be noted, with half of Gabriel's goodwill.

'What did you advise?' Thomas asks.

Balsam, Gabriel tells them. If the pain worsens a dabble of salt, a cake of clay to keep it covered. 'You know better than anyone that time is more often the solution than anything else.'

The vicar jolts at this, slapping his thigh in delight. 'It says something that my parishioners and your patients often require the same cure,' he says. 'Time heals, yes. And is the Lord not the most compassionate physician of them all?'

Gabriel nods in vigorous agreement, as though seated in a church pew, taking in a sermon. Thomas watches the vicar entertain the boy before the old man slouches back into his chair, apparently fatigued – perhaps growing tired of the costume he's put on for the common folk; ready to return to his debonair quarters, his hot-spiced wine, his fur-lined gown that will keep him warm as the sun sets. The whore he will beckon when he longs for company in the dark.

The fire is dying.

'Take your portion and leave the rest on the mantle,' Thomas tells Gabriel.

Gabriel does as he is told and the vicar stands.

'I'll follow the boy out,' the vicar says. 'Vespers in less than an hour.'

The vicar puts down his tea as Gabriel meddles with his hair, taking longer than usual to depart. Thomas turns in his chair to face him, sensing the boy's unease.

'The woman of the house is with child,' Gabriel says. 'They know you are the best at what you do. She seeks your assistance. If you might help her when the time comes.'

The room falls silent. The vicar looks down at the points of his shoes and Thomas recognizes, strangely, a bitter taste, that of the cedar, having quickened its way through his nostrils, settling in the back of his throat.

'And you told them rightly that I no longer perform such operations,' Thomas says.

'I did, sir.'

'That there are many midwives who are competent.'

'I told her this as well.'

'Very good.'

'Well!' The vicar looks up. 'Might I offer you my blessing, Thomas? Perhaps you are ready for that, at least.'

Thomas does not respond. The silence is a sour note on which the meeting ends, but the vicar does not flinch from it. He is used to such rejection.

'Then another time,' the vicar says.

'Yes, Father,' Thomas says, that last word awkward on his tongue. 'Another time.'

Thomas sleeps little, which is a bitter irony, for it was the deprivation of sleep that brought Rose to him in the first place. She had come to his door midday many months before, and he had hardly heard the knock beneath the bleating of a sheep being sheared behind his property (an annoyance so great he had locked himself upstairs in his study to find some peace with his tea). When he finally ventured down the stairs he came upon a woman no more than twenty. Her face was thin, her nose aquiline, and he could not make sense of the shade of her hair – red, or brown – for the sun struck it with the quality of an illusion, and with each angle in which she turned the color settled on a different shade. What he knew was that it was a beautiful brush of tangle upon her head, unwieldy in a manner he'd think beneath even a common woman, yet so unique against the typical fashion that it took on the appearance of the taboo. He wished, oddly enough, and against his judgment, to run his hand through it. Instead he invited her in.

'They say you are the best at what you do,' she said.

'No. The best tend to the king. But it is a task I plan to take up when called.'

'Such confidence.'

'It is only faith. The faith to believe that I might do God's work. To heal others.'

The woman was no longer listening, had taken to peering about as though her eyes could not accommodate the sights before her.

'You're blessed to live in such a home,' she said. 'And to live among those of us who have so little.'

His home was not as respectable as she made it out to be. The roof was sodden wood, liable to drip at the slightest hint of rain, instilling a dampness that kept him coughing through most seasons. Two stories, yes, but his bed was in his study, and the stairs to reach it creaked so loudly he thought it might wake the township. His garden, well, the garden was beautiful, bountiful with the herbs that filled his medicine, but she had no way of knowing this from where she stood now.

'It's wise to be amongst the people you treat,' Thomas told her.

'You do not treat those like me,' the woman told him, quite boldly. 'Only those with money to spare or wine to trade. Or else you'd have a line out the door.'

'Should I not charge for my time? It's how it must be.'

She said nothing to this.

'I must ask the same of you,' he said. 'To show me you have the means . . .'

There was a great hesitation that overtook her, as though forced into an indecent act, and yet she then slipped a hand into the lining of her shoe, rising up once more with coins fanned out between her fingers. Satisfied, he took her to the storeroom, which had a stool for his patients to sit, a chair where he might sit beside them. His instruments hung in a line like a butcher's tools, a bucket beneath, although he rarely had a reason to use anything more than a lance and a needle. Bloodletting was his chief operation. But he knew other remedies when necessary.

He took her temperature. She told him her name.

'Rose. Tell me what ails you.'

She spoke quickly, as though she had been waiting for this opportunity for some time. 'I cannot sleep. It is as though my mind acts without the consent of my body. It speaks to me endlessly, at all hours.'

'That is all?' Thomas asked her.

'What might that mean? I am expected to look after my father's home and yet I am so restless I can hardly stand. I wish for nothing more than a deep slumber, a few hours of rest, and yet it never finds me. If that is nothing to you, then you do not know the torture of the malady.'

A rat scurried by them, and although Thomas turned at the patter, Rose did not.

'My father was a fisherman,' Thomas told her. 'He woke at an hour when God Himself was at rest and took to the waters. I worried over him endlessly. Unreasonable worries. That his boat would sink. That a whale would eat him. I never fell back to sleep. I know exactly what you speak of.'

The room was windowless, and even without illumination he still managed to see her eyes beside his own, the disappointment vanishing from them. In her excitement she pinched her gown at the thigh, the wool catching, rising as she leaned forward, awaiting his instruction. The pale of her skin was light in the dark. This he remembers well.

'It will most likely pass on its own. If you wish to pay for it, I can present you a brew. A bit of bile, henbane, ground lettuce . . . there are other ingredients. You'll need to be watched as you take to rest. And then watched as you sleep to reverse any unmeant effects.'

'All night?' she asked him.

'I told you, it will most likely pass on its own. But this is an option.'

She stood up before he could. Her hand took his own, brittle as coarse cloth, and deposited the coin into his hand. The following night, she told him. She would come and be put to sleep.

B ut that was some time ago.

He now wakens to noises he once loved, noises that have come to haunt him – the rustling beside his pillow, the creak of the bed, the sound of readying breath against his ear. And then it is all gone, extinguished like a flame. He turns to face the absence beside him. The cock crows, then another, for there are more than one, and each must have their say. He dresses, and before long the front door rattles; the house groans in response.

'Sir?'

'A moment, Gabriel.'

Thomas dresses. Gabriel appears each morning just like this, often waking him, always arriving at the same early hour, his voice full of life and prepared to take on whatever the day might demand. The routine gives Thomas comfort. He comes down to greet him, and there is, for the first time in recent memory, an unordinary sight. Gabriel has a package tucked in the fold of his arm.

The young man's face is alight. His eyes are unsheathed and wide with anticipation. 'I've brought something for you.'

Thomas pauses at the bottom of the stairwell, struggling, with great effort, to weather the boy's zeal. After a bit of wine, perhaps. But now, upon waking . . .

'Sit,' Thomas tells him. 'Let me at least start a fire.'

'The weather is quite nice today. I'm sure it will reach us soon.'

'It's in the ritual, Gabriel. The comfort is in the ritual.'

For a moment, Thomas looks out the window, wondering where the boy gets his good cheer. A slurry of shit and piss rambles down the street from some place up the ways. The burgh, once lively with carts and beggars, merchants hawking their wares, town criers offering their declarations, now rests in total silence. The pestilence continues to claim more bodies than the warden's office can count. All but those like Gabriel and the vicar – those with a higher calling Thomas can make no sense of – hide inside their homes. Praying, he imagines, for death not to knock.

He sets the wood to burn and they both sit before the heat, the itch of the flame a tingle on Thomas's heels.

'How did you rest?' Gabriel asks.

'There is no easy answer to that question.'

Nor is there an easy response, it would appear, and so Gabriel simply puts the gift upon Thomas's lap, and Thomas looks upon the object as though it is a small animal on offer for examination – something he'd rather be rid of.

'Go on,' Gabriel says.

'I do not need any gifts,' Thomas says. 'A job well done is the only gift I ask for, and you deliver it daily.'

'It's my pleasure to bring this to you.'

'You know I do not accept such things, Gabriel. It's not personal. Not in the least. A good physician must be restrained from emotion. In our trade it is of the utmost importance.'

'But, sir –'

'Do not be foolish. Disease has taken half the town to the grave. Those beloved hens you keep might perish. Your wife and child might fall ill. Keep your money. Keep what is yours. I am fine. I want for nothing.'

Gabriel stares at him. The light has vanished from his eyes yet he does not quit looking at Thomas, searching for something, perhaps a sign of affection, and it is as he stares that he begins to open the package himself, the paper crackling, tearing away, revealing a wooden tea set – two saucers, two cups, a kettle with an etching on its side, the rod of Asclepius, the god of healing.

'My son made this for you,' Gabriel says. 'It cost no money. It is nothing more than a show of gratitude. For all you have done for the people here. For my family. I know your set is finer, that you would not even deign to drink from such a cup as this one, but I could not stop him from carving it.'

A tremor overtakes Gabriel's hand, waiting for Thomas to claim his gift, and Thomas thinks only of the day the boy first showed up at his door, trembling from the cold, mud upon his feet, rags for clothes, pledging to be his faithful servant, if only he would teach him his trade. To grant his wish was perhaps the last good deed he'd ever managed, the last deed attached to no financial gain, to no desire of his own – and now, to have such goodwill thrust before him, in the face of his true wickedness, is almost too much to bear. But he does it for Gabriel. He takes the tea set and stands.

'I will put the set in the kitchen,' Thomas says. 'Tell your son it is well made.'

He pauses once he reaches the kitchen, staring ahead at the washbasin, the small glimmer of light that strikes it from the window above. There is a knock at the door. A patient, perhaps. Gabriel stands, eager, and Thomas only nods.

'Costume on,' he says. 'See to what they need.'

That night, as with the one before, time resolves itself in familiar patterns: the warden's jangling keys note midnight, prayers at matins, the sordid moans of the miller's wife before the rooster sings its song. Thomas is awake for all of it, thinking once more of Rose.

She'd taken the brew and sat upon his bed speaking endlessly of her upbringing, her father's obsession with his farm, a rather unsuccessful plot of land that he tended to so closely that he still slept in the fields for many nights at a time, worried that another man might come to steal his crop – blind to the daughter he had at home. Her mother had died from the pox. Thomas sat in a chair at the foot of the bed, noting the time, waiting breathlessly for a pause that might note her fatigue, a droop at the shoulder, the whine of a yawn. When it did not happen, by midnight, he gave the instruction to at least lie back – to give sleep the chance to take possession over her.

She asked of his own childhood, and he spoke of his father's wish for him to be a fisherman – how he could hardly remove the hook from a cod without cringing at the animal's suffering.

'And yet you become a physician?'

'To heal is quite a different matter altogether. One could call it redemptive, even. To witness the body's failing. To see its recovery. Blessings bestowed by God.'

'I hear the pride in your voice.'

Thomas could only raise his shoulders in resignation. 'Perhaps pride is my vice. We all must have one, no?'

In the dark, leaning in, he believes he can see her lips turn up, the start of a smile.

Their voices carried through the night, a parrying of thought, of opinion; at two they ate through a bowl of figs, so lost in discussion, in their hunger, that they did not notice the first strike of sunlight creeping through the window hours later, and it was decided, right then, that she would return again. A different treatment. He would see to it that this one worked better than the brew.

'And if it does not?' she'd asked, rising up from bed, flattening her gown at the chest, at the legs.

'Then we will at least have good conversation.'

'The distraction is not the worst remedy.'

On this point, they agreed.

Thomas slept long into the following day, and when he rose, prepared a different brew, a mixture of lavender which he had in his cupboard, and valerian which he had fetched from the market. For other patients, he had no time. He'd never found love, more out of duty to his profession than any particular reason, and he had come to view the idea as just that, something for others, to be thought of, and sung of, and yet now this woman had claimed him in the matter of an evening, stirred the cauldron that was his heart, and he saw no reason to devote time to any human but this one. It did not matter, the whispers he heard: those of fever, ghastly buboes, great suffering, inching its way toward the burgh from neighboring villages. Prepare, the vicar had told him one visit, as God was inflicting another pestilence upon His people. And yet only gladness found him when the door sounded that night and signaled Rose's return. And when she came, he was prepared with fresh linens upon his bed, the brew on the nightstand, his chair seated bedside, closer than he'd placed it upon her previous visit.

'You should get comfortable,' Thomas told her.

And this time Rose stripped to her gown, the soft mounds of her breasts, the slopes of her thighs, so mesmerizing as to be like starlight in the sky, brilliant enough to pierce through the shadows of the dark and capture Thomas in a reverie so deep he could hardly breathe.

'Sit and drink,' he said.

When they spoke, Rose's voice struck Thomas from the bed like velvet on his skin. She spoke on the monotony of threading, and how it subsumed her every hour, and how the clothes she made hardly sold at market; how those she mended rarely left the customer satisfied; spoke then of her quarrels with her father, how he wished her to marry only to have her offspring serve his fields.

'Do you wish to marry?' Thomas asked.

'If the time has not passed me by, yes.'

'What would you look for?'

'A woman should not deign to be so choosy.'

'But if made to?'

She readied an answer and Thomas could hear his heart grow restless, the beating so loud he feared Rose might take note.

'A man with cause,' she said. 'A man of bravery, and passion, not unlike the one before me.'

Who is to say which hand found the other's first; how the bodies grew tangled, how their moans coalesced and rose up from the bed like smoke from a chimney, a signal of their bodies becoming one in the span of a single evening. The only clear thing, to Thomas, was that he had failed his duty, for Rose did not sleep for a moment, nor did he, and yet, for perhaps the first time, his failure felt like a success, for he knew then that he had found something greater than a cure to an ailment, and that if this did not help him find peace, and help Rose find tranquility, than there was little hope for either of them.

By the time they spoke of marriage, Rose's father had succumbed to the pestilence himself. So many suffered that to mourn them all would have made for a helpless proceeding. The streets smelled like an ossuary, and there were calls each day for Thomas's help, for Gabriel's help, and yet they had no cure to offer. It had all been tried – powdered staghorn, hot plasters, saffron potion: those who suffered all died in the same fashion. It became clear the sickness existed in the air, unseen, and perhaps it was only through divine providence, a favor granted to those who wished to help the poor and betrodden, that Thomas had not fallen ill himself. He began to stay inside, and from the window, sipping his tea, he could see the bodies, indescribable mounds, carted through the street. The warden had them burned at night, but so many died that by daybreak the burning carried on, the sun clouded by the smoke, the air so thick with death that many vomited upon stepping outside.

The sick knocked incessantly. Thomas refused to answer, knowing they had no money, and it was only Gabriel who volunteered his help, for, as he told Thomas, those who tend to the poor lend to the Lord, and who was Thomas to deny him his sense of duty to God? Such silliness, Thomas thought. But he did not protest.

Rose came to him again one night. She had been cleaning her father's home, having already sold the estate for a small pittance. The money would go to Thomas, for their wedding, what little ceremony there might be – the vicar had promised to bless them, when he found the time – and she would soon be his. And yet there was more news, and when she told him in the kitchen, he nearly fell to his knees. It was as though an altogether different woman stood before him – how had he not noticed the swelling of her ankles, her complaints of being dizzy, the sudden plumpness? Her cheeks were red from toil, from the work of the day, and yet they struck Thomas with the radiance of something holy.

He approached her slowly, placed a hand upon her shoulder in silence, another against her stomach, only to pull them both away when she spoke once more to him.

'I do not want it,' she said.

What did it feel like? As though a snake had crawled out from her hair and bit him where he stood.

He had bled an older man earlier in the day, a quart taken at the thigh, and the man's temper, his gruffness, had reminded Thomas of his own father in a manner so vivid that the image remained with him long after. He could still trace the smell of blood, that hint of copper, lingering in the air, and now he imagined his father watching from the corner of the kitchen disapprovingly, surveying this scene with disgust before vanishing once more.

'You wish to *harm* our child,' Thomas said. He took her shoulder, brought her chin to his own, her eyes to his, which only made her pull away, stubbornly casting her gaze upon the mug of water in her hand. 'To be so callous. When you have me at your side, no less. Not only as your husband but as your physician.'

'Who is the callous one?' she said. 'I saw my father die. Moaning, grasping at his sheets. And you have seen countless others go the same way. I will not let a newborn suffer. Let it face the darkness of the world. It is not right.'

Thomas was flummoxed. 'The darkness of the world? That child is a gift. A *light* in the darkness. What you speak of is nothing short of a miracle.'

Rose looked at him then. Wholly, and without end, for so long that Thomas himself felt it wise to look away.

'There are no miracles here,' she said.

The room fell silent. Thomas placed a hand upon her hair, letting it fall to her shoulder once more. Her neck arched, and he ran his fingers upon the skin.

'My bed will be for the three of us,' he whispered. 'If that arrangement is not for your liking . . .'

The smell of blood in the air was replaced by that of yeast, of sugar so rich it brought Thomas's mouth to water. The miller delivering his bread.

'Why do you not go get a loaf for us?' Thomas asked. 'It will go well with a stew.'

Rose merely nodded. Turning to Thomas, her hand out; her palm up in search for coin.

The vicar pays a visit. There are great gusts of wind outside, howls that sound like screams, screams held back only by the shutting of the door.

'I have excellent news,' the vicar says.

Thomas is already sitting with a small clutch of grapes in hand, examining the window before him, how it shutters and clacks when the door opens, even though the covers are made of thread. Something awry, as though born of sorcery.

The vicar sits across from him and his face slackens immediately at the sight of the teacup, the clumsy curvature of the wood, his hand pulling away as though it had splintered when he touched it. Thomas shrugs. 'I expected Gabriel back now,' he murmurs. 'His son made this tea set for me and I wanted to demonstrate my appreciation –'

'Forget the tea!' the vicar exclaims, taking a sip, setting it down. 'The *king*, Thomas. The king has summoned you.' The vicar, usually so concise with his words, begins to speak so excitedly that he is rambling, his voice high enough to sound juvenile. 'The king's physician has succumbed. May God bless his soul, yes, but his death is no tragedy. The poor fellow could hardly keep his hands still when feeling for a pulse. I volunteered your name immediately. I know you have been hesitant to return to your work, but the time is right.'

For reasons he cannot discern, Thomas has stood up. He is pacing. Walking to the kitchen.

'Thomas?' the vicar calls out.

But Thomas is staring out of the small glass panel situated beside his back door onto the little square plot he once called his garden; what is now nothing more than a patch of dirt. His plants overrun by dandelions, St John's wort, dusted over footprints of animals that have visited in the night. He has let no one back there. To do so would be to allow access to his thinking. How quickly the place that was once the source of his pride has wasted away into nothing more than lifeless mud – feed for worms.

'Thomas,' the vicar says once more, his voice carrying through the house. 'You must answer this test. Consider it God's destiny. Mind you, you will be richer than one might ever imagine. And we will see each other every day. There is no safer haven than the king's court –'

'Enough,' Thomas calls out, and when he turns, he can feel the blood pulse at his temple, the spit drive from his mouth. 'Nothing more than an old fool too sorry to see he will die along with the rest of them. Caught up in your false God, your money, the pathetic pride you find in your worthless position.' He laughs madly, heartily – when was the last time he laughed? – turns, his chest beating in rhythm with his step, and walks back to the parlor, staring at the vicar intently. 'To think you'll be *spared*. That *any* of us will be spared. That your sorry castle on the hill is any better than my own dwelling. I am not like you or the physician you speak of. I won't hear another word regarding this proposition.'

The bruising has already appeared: the old man quivers at the chin, stunned silent. His eyes, so soft – fragile things, broken and undone – land on the carpet. Immediately Thomas feels the cords of his heart go taut. He lowers his voice, shakes his head apologetically.

'I did not mean what I said,' Thomas says.

Yet it is done. Already the vicar has recovered. He is smiling, his arms trembling as he grips the arms of the chair to rise. The pain, Thomas thinks, is not the old man's, but transmuted from the injured voice he has just endured, the source of anger and rage that Thomas himself has delivered unto him. He realizes he has not harmed him; no, he has only shown his own weakness.

'Please, sit, sit,' Thomas says, but the vicar is done with sitting. He waves him off with the flutter of his hand. His smile is serene. It flows over the room like sunlight, and it is enough to blind Thomas, to make him cover his eyes from his own embarrassment.

'It was a mistake to ever ask,' the vicar says. 'You are at peace here . . .' The vicar turns, facing the window, facing the street, the emptiness and the smoke of the sky and the dusted rim of the sun that hums red behind it. The wind is rapping desperately at the door once more. 'And you are correct to think of the world as it is. For the tempest of the Lord is wrathful. It bursts upon the head of the wicked.' He does something strange, then: tapping his knuckles upon his own skull, repetitive thuds, one after the other. The old man's smile is wide. There is a grim lesson hidden behind the jest; Thomas can only imagine the vicar does this performance chiefly for the children of the church, and now has found his friend so unworthy, so simple himself, that this is all the instruction he ought to be left with.

'As a wicked man myself, I must face it also. With love in my heart, Thomas.'

The old man places a hand on his chest. He walks to Thomas, and Thomas allows his old friend to place his other hand upon his own chest, to trace his heart with his thumb, and the gesture is firm enough to draw the breath from Thomas's body, to make him buckle into a prayer, to see grace in the old man before him.

'I imagine you don't wish to be left with a prayer.'

The door opens. The door closes. Like a ghost has entered his home and left it just the same.

He has not slept for two nights. There have been knocks – women carrying children in their arms, sullied men in rags who wheeze loudly, their voices like the croaks of a frog. They do not know he can see them from his bedroom. He would open the door for Gabriel, but they are not Gabriel, and already he knows where the boy has gone – home. Wherever home is. (He berates himself for not having asked him before.) And why would he not escape this wretched place? Take to the roads and return from where he came. A place of tranquility, where wide-hipped mothers carry their infants in slings and need only nurse them to good health when sickness strikes; a place where men hunt in the morning and roast their prey at night, laughing in a circle with the others, saliva on their lips and drink in their hands.

Gabriel will shepherd them to his God. He will bring the Good Book and they will bow to it, and he will be their vicar, their doctor, their everything. Bile rises from Thomas's throat, and he senses the imbalance in his own person, the sickness upon him, and he rises finally, disgusted by his envy. He goes downstairs, the stairs speaking to him in that familiar string of thuds and moans. It is cold, but he does not start a fire, and, as though his body has been overtaken by a spirit, his feet lead him not to his chair but rather to his garden. The smell of the coffee, coarse and bitter, mixes with the smell of the soil, an odor that has risen from the morning fog and gathered in the air. It was here he took Rose in his panic, after the sheets upon their bed had grown so soiled in blood and feces and sweat that it formed a puddle in the dimple of the floor beside his mattress. She had asked for a midwife before the birth, howled for one during, and yet his belief in his own skill was total. For was he not the attendant so many mothers sought when their midwives had failed? And yet this child – his own child – eluded him. The proximity of it, and its vexing position, presented itself as a perversity: the soft slope of its bottom, doughy at the touch yet firmly entrenched against Rose's opening, was like the sight of a miracle glimpsed. To pull him out by force was to risk Rose's life. Yet the child would not survive left like this. It needed to be turned, and yet Thomas could not manage, could not quite reach the place required. To touch Rose's stomach, to try to access the child's form, caused her to moan so loudly that he feared she had been possessed. He felt utterly confused, utterly useless. He began to pray then, to Saint Margaret, the saint of childbirth, and finally to God, pleading for help as his own body began to tremble, as he saw, quite truly saw, the life leaving Rose's body, her skin turning from pale to diaphanous, the legs slack, her eyes empty, and although he had seen death before he had not been so close to it by way of his own soul, his own love, and he fell from the birthing stool and cried so deeply that he thought his wife's pain had entered his own being. He was sure of it then. His jaw was agape at the scene before him, the death and the horror, the blood pattering onto the floorboard so loudly he could hear it between his sobs, a rattling, like the hum of those praying at Mass, like thunder rolling through the church.

It was Gabriel who would find him; Gabriel who would clean up the gore while humming a hymn, wrapping Rose in linen, the child buried within her. How calm the boy was, as though Rose's was the corpse of any other lost patient. Thomas had taught him to demonstrate this tranquility, a means to ease the pain of grieving loved ones, and only now did he realize how wrong his instruction had been. How false it rang. And yet he could not rise up and condemn Gabriel as he wished. Could not leave the corner where he hugged his knees to his chest. A boy in fear.

'This body is only a vessel, Thomas,' Gabriel had said. 'You know this as well as I do. Yet the afterlife is eternal. And one day you will meet her there. Shall I fetch the vicar for you? Say only the word and I will go.'

But to say anything would be to break the spell. To begin the procession of the present becoming the past. So he sat silently. Staring at his failures, his loss; knowing now that God had abandoned him; certain, then, that He would do the same with all His people in time.

The vicar has been gone for some time now. Thomas brews tea and takes his place in the parlor beside the fireplace. The house is so quiet that he thinks to say something, to speak to himself, but this corresponds to what must be the first seedling of some avenue of madness, and so he decides to keep quiet. He is so still that he cannot fathom to move his hand from the teacup in his hands, cannot even look down to see the rod of Asclepius, for he would think not only of his failures as a man of medicine, but as a husband, as a friend, as a father. He imagines what he must look like, frozen here, alone as the world trembles and its people die, and this, he decides, is a sort of loneliness that is worse than the fate of those who have passed.

A knock at the front door. The wood shakes lightly, and it is in the briskness of the tapping, the way it recedes so quickly, politely, that he knows who it is.

'Gabriel?' he calls out, standing at once. He feels blood flowing through him again. 'Where have you been?' he asks, walking closer to the door.

'Sir,' Gabriel says, and his voice, even muffled by his mask, is so weak that Thomas stops suddenly where he is.

A single cough, then. Wet, phlegmatic; a curse unchained.

'Oh,' Thomas says.

'I was tending to a young woman with a foot so swollen she could not stand. I felt a wracking in my chest. It is not at its worst yet.' His voice is light and airy, even cheery, as it sounds every morning. Thomas does not know what to say. He takes a hand from the saucer and peels back the drapes. The beak of Gabriel's mask stares back at him menacingly. As if on cue the boy removes it altogether, and Thomas wonders, considering the result of this decision, if he is purposefully trying to gain his pity.

Gabriel is pallid, his eyes sunken into his skull, but otherwise there is little to glean from his features. There is nothing Thomas wants more than to invite him in. To have company for even a moment, a distraction from the cries he hears at night, the dark skies, the empty parlor.

'I wonder,' Gabriel says, his voice catching, 'if I were to keep my distance . . . I cannot go home. I cannot see my family. But perhaps we can try a new powder. I had some ideas, untested. If you have some cabbage. A bit of henbane . . .'

They are staring at one another in a manner that is foreign to them both. A helplessness seems to tether them to this spot, and yet both now seem to be at a loss to say more. The boy will die. He knows he will die. And Thomas cannot help him, for he cannot help anyone, not even himself, and knowing this, knowing full well how little there is to be done, he can think of nothing more than to raise the teacup in his hand, like some child showing off his toy. His hand shakes terribly. There are tears in his eyes.

'Look at that!' Gabriel says, clasping his hands together. 'My son will be so happy to know you are making use of the tea set. What a pleasant surprise.'

There is a question of who is administering to whom, for it is clearly Thomas who appears to be suffering the most, unable to utter a single word. And Gabriel smiles as he does, forever content, even before his own death, knowing full well he will never see his son or tell him of this man, this supposedly great man, who has made use of his shoddy teacup.

Thomas puts a hand to the window. He imagines it against the boy's chest – as though he can feel his heart pumping, that throb, that swelling, that endless fount of energy and life that makes him a physician of such skill. He then pulls it away as quickly as he placed it there.

'I can wait,' Gabriel says, 'If you simply wish to unlock the door and let me in. Thomas, please.'

He places the teacup on the desk beside his chair. He wants to tell him so much: that he is the best physician he has ever known. That he is like a son to him. That there is a life after this one, ever eternal, and he has nothing to fear.

But he says none of this. Only gives the boy one more look, hoping all he wishes to say is somehow related in his gaze. He lets the drapes fall against the window. Takes a step back. Retreats, upstairs, to pray for the world entire. ■

THE

WHITE

REVIEW

'Nothing less than
a cultural revolution'
Deborah Levy

THE EMPEROR CONCERTO

Julie Hecht

I was wondering about Beethoven's state of mind when he wrote the 'Emperor' Concerto. Because it has an endless end – and endless ending. And I'm sure that musicologists and scholars have written about the insanely beautiful part known in music as rondo. But I'm too tired to look that up. I was wondering if he was going mad when he wrote the concerto because when I listened and watched for the third time on the annoying YouTube, with 'Ads' and 'Skip Ads' interrupting, I thought this rondo is going to drive me mad. It's never going to end. And I looked at the pianist, Mitsuko Uchida, half magical princess, half wild being. While I listened to the unbelievable beauty of her playing – delicate and light-handed, but strong and filled with passion – I realized that compared to her and Seiji Ozawa, we're all little pipsqueaks. And to think my husband prevented me from seeing them perform at Carnegie Hall and in Boston, and at Tanglewood, and it's too late now because Ozawa is so frail and Mitsuko might be less energetic now. She might not be able to fly off the bench, throwing her aquamarine organza sleeve with her delicate white-skin arm into the air.

I looked at her. She was wearing a blue-green organza blouse with a crinkly – is it *ruched*? – camisole underneath, her beautiful, white, smooth skin showing. It was distracting, the sleeves were so big and puffy, and you could see her arms and slight, thin chest through the middle tighter part. She hadn't had her hair blown dry straight. Hair blow-drying is a waste of life. Her hair was cut in thick layers and it was wild. She was like a wild woman when she played, and I wondered how she could play that way without going crazy. And then I looked at Ozawa, and the rondo wasn't bothering him. I guess he'd done it many times before and he knew the music-history explanation for it. Then I remembered my piano teacher from childhood. One day he said, 'How would you like to play a little Gershwin for a change?'

'How about Beethoven? The Moonlight Sonata,' I said.

'You know Beethoven was blind and deaf when he wrote that.'

And since I was only eleven, I said, 'Oh no. How come? Why?'

The piano teacher said, 'He had syphilis.'

'What's that?' I said.

Then he called my mother in from the kitchen where she was holding an orange Le Creuset pot, for those onions, as usual. I mean, how could it be so important for my mother always to be cutting onions in the kitchen?

He asked her, 'Doesn't anyone tell this kid anything?'

'Tell her anything like what?'

And he said, 'Well, she doesn't know what syphilis is.'

'She's only eleven,' my mother said. 'Why should she know about that?'

'We were talking about Beethoven,' he said.

He was kind of a bohemian, now called hip, but somewhat overweight guy. He wore corduroy suits and dark blue shirts with olive-green ties. He used to come and smoke a cigar and let my mother feed him every fattening thing she had cooked and baked the whole week. During my piano lesson he would show me how a piece of music ought to be played and he would explain by singing along with Mozart, and instead of saying, 'la la la', or 'la da', like most people, he would sing 'ya ba ba' and 'ya ba bom' and 'bom bom pom', and more and more excitedly 'ya pa pom! pa pa pom!', rocking back and forth and bouncing up and down in the antique chair my mother had provided for him until I thought the seams of his corduroy pants and the buttons on his hopsack cloth shirt would pop off from the pressure. I was afraid the veins standing out in his face would burst and that his whole person might just explode from the exertion.

He was married to a beautiful modern dancer. She was thin and had creamy white skin and long black hair she wound up and stuck at the top of her long neck with big, tortoiseshell hairpins and she had thick bangs. They were an arty and elegant couple. She was arty and elegant, anyway. He was arty.

I pictured the room. I pictured sitting at the piano on the bench, with these beautiful pink roses on the dark green needlepoint cover. We bought the piano from an older couple in their apartment, with the needlepoint cover bench. To think I was offered that bench when my parents sold our house, and I didn't take it. My apartment had two rooms, without space for the piano or the bench. I would like to look at that bench so much. The bench could be opened up and inside were all the yellow Mozart piano books. If only I could be in that room with those many big windows looking out onto what's called a tree-lined street, and inside, walls of shelves of books and my mother in the doorway with her orange-red Le Creuset pot, and my teacher sitting in a chair next to the piano.

Once, in an argument with the teacher, he pushed me at the bench to show feeling and I refused to play after that. He said, 'Do you hold that against me?' I said, 'Yes, you pushed me at the piano bench. You're not supposed to do that. I don't understand how you can have such a beautiful, wonderful wife.' He was amused, and he said, 'Well, how is she so beautiful?' And I said, 'Oh everything, her hair. That long thick black hair. That white skin. That beautiful big smile.' And he said, 'But you have the same long hair. And yours is blonde.' And I said, 'Oh, but hers is thicker. She has those thick bangs. She's just so beautiful and everything she has is beautiful.' And he said, 'Well, why do you suppose she married me?'

'I don't know,' I said. 'But it was a mistake or some error in judgment.' He was entertained by that. I guessed he knew he was a lucky man.

I could tell that the teacher didn't like me. He was brought in to make my older sibling feel better. He was told how she felt so bad because she was not attractive or entertaining. However, even she was entertained at the dinner table when I told stories of what I'd seen and done that day. They even laughed at imitations of their table manners. And all the attention from everyone we knew or met went in my direction. Then the piano teacher was filled in, as so many people were, with that sob story. That's why he preferred the evil sibling.

I couldn't help that I looked like a movie star and made people laugh – I thought all children's looks were equal and I chose my friends because they all looked different. I couldn't help it that I was born and that my older sibling never got over it. That's why she was miserable and depressed. My mother did everything to keep me down.

A Viennese child psychoanalyst told me, when I was a young grown-up – and she wasn't an empathetic person – 'I have seen one child completely destroyed to protect the other.'

About thirty years later I was friendly with a precocious pre-teenaged son of a world-renowned reproductive surgeon, who said to me, 'I have a way on my computer where I can find anyone. Do you want me to find someone?'

'Yes, find my piano teacher,' I said. 'Ivan Fiedel. Find him.'

A bit later that evening the boy reported back to me that he had found the piano teacher, his phone number and where he lived in California.

He offered to call him for me.

When he reported back, he had a long story to tell. He said the teacher talked and talked and talked and talked. And he added, 'You know what, he didn't like you. He just liked your older sibling. He just wanted to ask about her.' The boy thought it was funny. I could tell he was smiling.

The piano teacher told the boy everything about his life, that he'd had an illness and for a while he didn't think he'd recover. But he did recover. The boy said, 'The stories he told, he went on and on and on! He couldn't stop talking about your whole family, your parents, your sibling, your house! Early-American antiques bought inexpensively. Art that had been given. But the main thing is, I could tell he didn't like you.' He was still amused.

I said, 'That's right, he didn't. He once pushed me as I was playing and he yelled, "Move! Move! Move!" Then he added, "Marion Greene moves around with feeling when she plays these sonatas! You're not supposed to sit there like a wooden stick."'

He probably wished he'd had Mitsuko Uchida as his student. It's possible, she was much younger than he was but she lived in Vienna at the time. Who was her teacher? I guess I could google it, but it would take too long.

I had the courage to say, 'I think Marion Greene looks like a complete fool when she moves around. I don't want to be like that. I'm just playing the piano. I do what she does when I'm imitating a famous pianist I've seen on TV. Everyone laughs.'

He liked it when I explained this because he considered that one of his side points as a piano teacher was getting adolescents to express their true inner feelings and solve their hidden conflicts. Emotional outbursts were fine with him. I used to pretend to be wildly conducting a symphony or even playing a sonata. My mother and aunt found this funny, laughing their heads off, instead of just sending me to the High School of Performing Arts. My high school was more like one in Beverly Hills.

My mother said he'd told her that Marion was learning like a house on fire, and then said to me, in her meanest way, 'You're learning like a house not even started.'

Years later I wished the teacher could know that I had Mozart's complete works and listened all the time. I saw him interviewed on TV one year, running a progressive music and dance school in Connecticut, and then I saw his wife buying a black cape and black coat on the designer floor at Lord & Taylor. She looked exactly the same, twenty years later, the same exact face, the same black hair, no gray and not dyed; maybe a few lines around the eyes from laughing and being happy and hip. I told her who I was and she didn't remember if I had my name or my sibling's. She said her baby was fifteen now and a very sensitive boy.

When I was about eleven and I told the piano teacher I hated the boring Hannon piano exercises, he said, 'How would you like to take a little vacation from Hannon?' I was quick to agree and when he never resumed them after three years I didn't remind him, although it was always on my mind.

Once, after he got me to confess that I sometimes hated my mother, he said, 'How would you like to talk to a psychiatrist?'

'But I'm not crazy.'

'You don't need to be crazy. Lots of people do it if they're a little confused the way you are.'

'What does a little confused mean?'

'It means I know lots of people who feel better after they go to one.'

'Including you?'

'People like me.'

He'd probably been going for years and was still going. I didn't know that part of society yet.

'And kids your age,' he added.

'What?'

'Yes. Lots of kids like you.'

'Anyone I know?'

'My brother.'

'What brother?'

'My kid brother.'

'You have no brother, no young brother.'

'Sure I do. He's fifteen.'

'But you're old.'

'How old am I?'

'In your thirties.'

'I'm thirty-six and my parents had a surprise baby when I was twenty.'

'Is that why he's crazy?' This is something I might have said as Lolita in the film version of *Lolita*. I love the moments when she screams at James Mason, 'You're crazy!' I could have played that part of dialogue, although the unbelievably great performance of the teenage actress Sue Lyon was perfect for all of the movie. I was too high class to play that character.

'Wait a minute. He's not crazy. He had some problems, he got some help and now he's getting straightened out. He's a lot happier kid now, less guilty, less withdrawn, more in touch with life.' That was his style of talking.

'Uh-huh,' I said. Even then I didn't care for that style.

'Are you interested in looking into it?' the teacher asked.

'I don't believe you have a brother that age.'

'Why not?'

'You never said so before.'

'It never came up.'

'You're always telling about all the kids you know, especially ones that you've helped with their mental problems.'

'I didn't get to help him, the psychiatrist did.'

'I'll ask your wife. She wouldn't make something up like that.'

'Why would I if she wouldn't?'

'She's superior to you.'

'Ha. Really? How?'

'She's beautiful and thin and kind. She doesn't interfere with people's minds. She'd never scream and push a student over at the piano.'

'You hold that against me still?'

'Always.'

The piano teacher and his beautiful dancer wife had two little children. A photo of her had appeared in *Life* magazine just after she had her first baby by natural childbirth, in the delivery room with what looks like all her stage makeup still on, smiling in ecstasy with her new baby. My mother said, 'It's not normal for a man to talk about details of natural childbirth. This is what women talk about, amongst themselves.'

This was the beginning of the new era. I guess he was ahead of his time, or her time anyway. Now everybody talks about everything.

In the photograph the dancer-wife looked beautiful and not even tired. But my mother didn't want to hear about that either – the fact there was no anesthesia used and maybe she went home the next day or the same day. Hard to remember every detail.

My mother would bring out those samples of unhealthful things she was cooking in the kitchen. The piano lessons were mostly about her giving him samples of food she was cooking for dinner, in fact about anything other than the piano playing. Antique furniture was another topic.

It's not as if I were a great piano student. Chopping onions was always more important than anything. And I hate everything about onions. I begged her not to cook onions during the daytime, especially in the morning. Not a good aroma for waking up, not like toast.

When I was four, and we lived in an old, antique-filled house in Brooklyn, a part that's become hip and fashionable now – luckily I have a photograph of the room of the scene I remember – my mother was in the kitchen doing something, and while we were arguing, I was telling her over and over that I had nothing to do. She finally lost her temper and followed me into the living room with that long, pointy knife she had for cooking big things. She might have been screaming, 'You're the curse of my life. What did I do to deserve this?' This scene caused hysterical crying on my part. I lay on the couch, face down, in wild hysteria.

During the middle of the crying, my closest friend, who lived in the house next door, came and knocked on the door. It was a glass French door inside the vestibule. It had a thin white curtain over it, the way it was done. My mother asked her in, but I still couldn't stop crying.

My friend said, 'What's wrong? Why is she crying like that?'

And my mother said, 'Oh, some little thing. Come in.'

But my friend was so terrified that she left. Or was it that my friend stayed and we tried to talk for a minute first? Because a little later, my mother came back into the room, still in her housedress with an apron – I wish I could remember which ones – and she said, 'But why were you so hysterical? Things like this have happened before.'

'You had a knife,' I said.

'You thought I was going to attack you?'

'You were holding it and screaming.'

And she said, with what looked like regret and guilt, 'I just happened to have the knife in my hand. If I had a cup, I would have come in there with a cup.' I always remember this sentence exactly the way she said it.

Upon review of the scene, she meant a measuring cup. But I pictured a white teacup, the simplest, plainest kind in children's books. It still didn't make sense. I tried to understand the scene, but I couldn't be sure because of the idea of the cup. Also there was the screaming, 'You're the curse of my life,' when she came into the living room. I had heard that before. Just because I had said I had nothing to do. She hadn't arranged anything the way other mothers did.

She probably told my father about the incident when he came home from work. They must have both been sad. Maybe my mother cried.

I complained to my mother that I didn't like the piano teacher's behavior one of the times when she was raving about what an 'unusual guy' he was and how lucky we were to have him instead of the average kind of piano teacher. That's what my parents get for moving to a suburb, they lost their perspective of quality. There must have been a million of his type in Manhattan. Now I see my mother was right. I understand him better and wish we all could have stayed friends.

'He's not a psychologist,' I said. 'He's just here to give piano lessons.'

'How do you know he's not a psychologist?' she said in her mean way.

It always worried me after that, that he was a secret psychologist and just pretended he was there to give piano lessons.

Before this guy, we had an old-fashioned strict-style piano teacher. We went to her apartment for piano lessons. She was a middle-aged kind of piano teacher with short curly hair, with some gray in it. She insisted that we hold our elbows up high, higher than our hands, to play anything on the piano.

When I told the hip piano teacher about this, he said, 'Oh, I know about her. She's damaged a lot of kids.'

I wish I knew what happened to these people. I wish I knew their whole life stories. I guessed it was a coincidence that her niece taught ballet lessons.

That was all I knew.

My idea for a spring day was to get a ride in a convertible. Walking was not yet known. The piano teacher had an old white Chevrolet convertible and when he saw how surprised I was that he had the top down he offered to take me for a ride.

'Is there some great maternity shop around here?' he asked my mother. 'I'd like to pick up some surprise present for the mother-to-be.'

'Maternally Yours!' I said. 'I've always wanted to go there!'

'You have, huh? Why have you?' He was looking at me intently.

'They have such cute things in the window. Like Lucille Ball wears in *I Love Lucy*.'

'I hope they're better than the name of the place. Is it any good,' he asked my mother.

'It's supposed to be. I don't know really, I've never been inside.'

'I always try to get her to go,' I said.

'But we have no reason to. I don't want people to see us going in there. You don't just go browsing in a maternity shop for no reason.'

'Well I have a reason,' the piano teacher said. 'Let's go.'

When we got to the shop and parked across the street he said, 'I'll be out in ten minutes.'

'Can't I go with you?'

'Nah, you better wait here. I don't want them to think I'm buying it for you.'

'How could they?'

'I don't want to take any chances. Better wait outside in the car.'

'Can I look in the window?'

'That'd be worse. I'll be right out.'

In just a few minutes he came back carrying a giant white box tied with royal-blue ribbon. It was like the movies where the husband goes in for a present and spends lots of money very easily after seeing only one or two things. I've never gotten a package wrapped in a white box with a ribbon and then jumped into a convertible and happily zoomed away. I had to have admiration for the piano teacher the way he did that, even if he was a little overweight.

When my mother took my sister for college interviews, the piano teacher came for a lesson. He asked where my mother was. I told him, 'They're at Wellesley for a college interview. And Tufts.'

'Why didn't you go too?' he asked.

'My mother said I was too young and I would get in the way of important things they had to do.'

'But you might want to go to Wellesley some day.'

I didn't think of that.

I liked Smith better. There was more grass, more ivy – there were more bricks. There was an inn with an antique spinning wheel in the main floor and four-poster canopy beds upstairs. I liked Smith better mainly because it had more ivy. I judged colleges by the amount of ivy, bricks, green grass, beautiful old trees. I didn't know that's why these colleges were called the Ivy League, and Seven Sisters schools. Even after I'd seen all the ivy. I thought it was just a name. I thought there were only three colleges: Smith, Wellesley, and what they called Mount Holyoke at the time. I didn't count Radcliffe because there was hardly any lawn, or brick, and hardly any ivy. I couldn't take it seriously. This is before I knew about Bennington. But when I went for the interview all the girls seemed depressed and boy-crazy.

When we went to visit Smith, we stayed at that beautiful, antique inn with the antique spinning wheel. A kind, New England-style older lady, who appeared to be the manager of the inn, asked me, 'Are you here for an interview and to see Smith?'

I said, 'No, my older sister is here for an interview.'

She smiled and said, 'Well, you may want to come here, too, someday.'

I'd never thought of that, either. I thought colleges were for older teenagers and my place was just in my room, listening to Elvis Presley on my pink radio. I still had a carton of Little Lulu comics under my bed.

The night of the Wellesley trip, the teacher said, 'So you're left alone with your father? What are you two going to do?' My father didn't pick up on the father–daughter stuff. He didn't think girls were serious and he showed no emotion.

'Well, we went to dinner at a Chinese restaurant,' I said.

There were no good restaurants in suburbs during that era. Even in the city, just the fancy French ones. We often had to go to Longchamps, a dark and dreary formal restaurant on the ground floor of the Empire State Building with a menu consisting of things like turkey, or mashed potatoes, canned cranberry sauce – not just for Thanksgiving, but all the time. My mother always found this to be the only thing to order. She would ask me, 'How is that? Is that any good?'

'Not too good. Canned string beans,' I would say. And she would say, 'I thought so. Most restaurants aren't good.'

When I remember this, I'm surprised she was asking my opinion about food, since, as a vegetarian, there was hardly any food I could order and there was hardly any food she didn't like. I was a vegetarian at an early age when I found out most food was some kind of animal.

During my lesson I was tired and kind of slumped over as I played my Mozart sonata, and finally the teacher said to my father, 'What'd you do to this kid, get her drunk?'

'She only had a couple of sips.'

'Well, let's give this up until next week,' the teacher suggested.

'She only had the orange from my whiskey sour,' my father said. 'That couldn't have much effect.' I felt sorry for my father. He seemed guilty, as if he really thought he'd done something wrong.

'I'm just naturally tired,' I said. Life was tiring.

During the dinner we never spoke, maybe just a few sentences. When he did, it was about history or current events. He ordered that whiskey sour and offered me some. First I ate the orange and the carcinogenic red cherry and then I had a few sips. It was like some interesting orange juice. My father was thinking about something serious. I could tell. Then we came back for the evening piano lesson. I guess it was spring, there was daylight savings, so we had to have dinner early.

My father didn't seem to like me either. He could talk to my sibling because she was scholarly. She had no friends. She stayed in her dreary, blue-green room, always alone, reading. I liked to be outside playing with my friends or studying the insides of their houses.

He'd talk to her about history, but I was interested in Elvis Presley. What could we say about him?

The name of the restaurant was the Joy Inn. But all the times we went there I don't remember any joy – only my father's admonition not to eat spare ribs, or any greasy, unhealthy, disgusting thing on the menu. What could be more disgusting than spare ribs? I guess there are many things. Just think about the pigs, and their treatment, ending up on a plate.

I can still see the spare ribs shining right now, under the orange sugar marinade. A vegan even then, my dinner was the sloppy dish called vegetable chow mein or even sloppier Buddha's Delight – not a delight. I bet Jacqueline Kennedy and Caroline were never taken to places like the Joy Inn.

Upbringing is important, and I've never gotten over mine.

While the two conspirators were away at Wellesley, I discovered that my best slip was missing from my drawer. My drawers were neat in those days. When things needed repairs my mother had them done, when they were old and worn, she took them for rags. When things were outgrown, they were given away. Not the way it is now, the drawers are now with sections and areas of indecision, which gradually become mixed in with those I use until I can't tell which is which or what things are there for in the first place.

My mother organized everything: socks, underwear, slips and nightgowns. This slip was nylon. It was a color called powder blue, with scallops of white lace at the hem, and there was a little flower embroidery at the top of each scallop. I saved it for special occasions.

When the evil twosome got home from the college tour, I asked my mother, 'Where is my blue slip?' She helped me look. She was only fifty-percent evil.

'Did you look all through your drawer?' she said.

'Yes,' I said. 'Look, it isn't here.'

And then she said, 'Maybe ____ took it.'

I kept turning things over in the drawer and looking into my nightgown and sock drawers. I was late for school that day and when I asked my mother about the slip, she said again, 'Maybe ____ took it.'

I said, 'How could she take my best slip? She has her own. She's older. It's not even her size! It's small! She wears medium! I'm only eleven!' Maybe I was almost screaming by then.

It turned out that she had taken it. My mother asked her, and she said none of hers were clean. Typical – always taking my things because hers weren't clean, and for other, deeper reasons.

I believe I screamed at her, 'You probably stretched it out with your wide hips!'

'Cut it out now,' my mother said. A favorite thing of hers to say.

'She always asks for my best thing and then she uses it for slopping around. She wears silk to fry food and wash pots.'

To this very day she tries to steal from me. I was glad she was only on the waiting list at Wellesley. I wished I had remembered to say, 'God punished you for stealing my blue slip.'

There were three people chosen to try out for our grammar school graduation program. There was a talented piano player who was going on to Juilliard and he was known to be the one who would win. And then there were two others. There was me, because it was known I could play classical music, Mozart sonatas. I think it was known because they just asked in a haphazard, uncaring way: 'Who can play the piano? Who can play classical music?' And then there was a third person. But it was assumed that the Juilliard-headed student was going to be the winner.

I mentioned to my piano teacher that this was coming up, and he said, 'Oh, why don't you play the second movement of the Mozart sonata that you learned.'

And I just said, 'OK. But really, he's the pianist and he's known to be the one.'

My piano teacher said, 'I know, but why don't you try?'

'I'm not a talented pianist,' I said. 'I'm a writer, and an actress. I'm a storyteller.'

'Why don't you compete?'

'Oh, because it's for him,' I said. Anyway, I'd be too fearful to be competitive.

The truth is, he was a little nerdy guy. He had the appearance of something called a schlemiel. He shrugged a lot. He was short. He was cute in a way, in that Eastern European way. And certain girls liked him. He was kind of a mess. His shirts were always crumpled up and hanging out of his pants on the side. He was in his own world of musical practicing. Years later I met an English psychiatrist with that shirt style. He was outside at night in a parking lot, calling, 'I can't find some papers!'

At the audition, when I played the sonata in the stick-of-wood style – my mother didn't come. She was probably home chopping onions or in Manhattan at her other favorite store, Ohrbach's, where women could get low prices on designer clothes, not as great as Loehmann's. Next she'd probably be meeting my father for dinner and going to a play. My mother really couldn't care at all about my activities. She once took me into that store with her. It was packed with women five inches from each other. My mother was wearing a black velvet, corduroy wide-wale hat she had been saving from the 1940s. It came to a slanted point on top and near the point in one place there was a small collection of tiny gold bells. My mother, who usually had the best taste in everything including clothing, said to me, 'Now if we get separated from each other, just listen for the little bells ringing.' She couldn't have believed I could hear those tiny bells ringing in that mob scene. No wonder I was a terrified child, and grown-up too.

Since this piano student was the talented pianist and I had different talents, I was surprised at the silence and then applause after I played. The students looked at me in this way: 'Oh, she can play the piano, too?' And they applauded more. And then I just got up and I went back to my seat, knowing the Juilliard boy had to win. And he did. And that was fine with me.

I was surprised that my piano teacher wanted me to compete with a serious musician. I guess he was an early feminist. He didn't know the Juilliard student. He probably would have liked to have been his teacher, but the boy had a special Juilliard teacher. Some years ago I saw an album he had recorded. He was wearing a tuxedo and he had white hair. He had become an important pianist.

In an interview, I heard Mitsuko was mad for Beethoven. She's supposed to be a Mozart lover, known for her unique interpretations of Mozart. I'd read in the interview with her that she was mad, mad, mad for Beethoven.

I fell into another deep state of gloom and barely remembered Mitsuko and her performances. The world health and political crises were worsening. Then I saw her being interviewed again. I heard her say, 'I don't know why people don't go to concerts anymore. That's not what I mean.' She meant something else. That wasn't the subject here. I missed that part. She sounded annoyed.

I didn't know people didn't go to concerts anymore. Classical music concerts. I thought only I didn't go, because I didn't live near Carnegie Hall or any of the places there were classical piano concerts, especially Mozart and Beethoven.

The only ones I'd ever seen in recent years were in a Nantucket Congregational Church. It wasn't air-conditioned, and I always sat in the last seat of the last row, near the open window. Hot humid air was coming through, and I needed my personal battery-powered fan in order to stay without fainting. I have several little powerful fans, but you can't really take them to a concert. People in the other rows are disturbed by the noise, especially the fastest setting #3.

The humidity and the BBC World News, bad parts skipped, watching the whole thing in five minutes still interfered with the nights of obsession with Mitsuko and the 'Emperor' Concerto.

Yes, I had been mad for Beethoven, but now I was just mad. ∎

Akwaeke Emezi

what if mary auntie called me on my birthday

'i hear you're not talking to your mother,' she says, and her voice is a slippery crush of green olives, a sweet fig, patient and centuries old, i never ask about her birthdays anymore, 'is it because he's married?' she asks, 'or is this the one who had the baby? i've lost track.'

none of them, but she thinks all my heartbreaks are connected, 'i'm so tired,' i tell her, 'i don't want to talk to the start of summer or her loud wonders.' all the love letters sound the same, all the men think they're special, i buy my own selling spiels, i mean them all, i am so bored

'i remember when my son was like this,' she says, 'have you been to the desert? little gods like you always have to go.' i try to guess what is at her end, wine or weaving, a bird or bread, a flaming sunset

'in and out,' i reply, 'you know how it is.' the gaping fall, the rotting manna, the gush of final salvations, the hills, the caves, so much dies out there. mary auntie sighs and a flock of sparrows crashes against my ear

'how old are you by now,' she asks, and my hands grow sandy fault lines as i try to count. 'i've forgotten,' i confess, her voice creaks through the phone like latticed wood, like a dark cube, 'me too,' she whispers. 'me too.'

THE LONDON MAGAZINE

Where literary heritage meets the best in new writing

Discount Code: GRANTA

Granta readers can receive 15% off our Classic, Premium and Gift Subscriptions
Simply enter the code above at checkout

CHRIS HOARE
Usher, originally from London, flexes in the last light on Stapleton Road, Bristol, 2021

AN OLIVE GROVE IN ENDS

Moses McKenzie

1

> Look at the birds of the air, for they neither sow nor
> reap nor gather into barns; yet your heavenly Father
> feeds them. Are you not of more value than they?
> – Matthew 6:26

This is a story, much like any other, of ends and beginnings. Like any story, it is hard to know where to begin. But I think it makes sense to start at home, or a home. Actually, it might be more accurate to call it a house; one that stood alone atop Mount Zion, overlooking Leigh Woods, the Avon Valley and the muddy river that wound beneath.

'Dis is the yard,' I told Cuba, as we waited at its bourn, 'the one man's marge showed man when man was a young buck.'

The Bath stone house in the area known as Clifton was all original features; sash windows and working shutters. It had a vestibule and behind it a long plot of land that tripped and fell into the woods like the Hanging Gardens of Babylon. It could have been plucked from a fairy tale about two adventurers who had stumbled across the City of God. The front of the house was gated, guarded by statuette men from all nations clothed in white robes and carrying palm fronds.

And in the middle of the driveway sat a fountain of living water.

'It's rah massive,' Cuba said. And I understood his astonishment. It was a world away from the one we knew. Even if we owned the yard next to Nanny's and knocked it through, it wouldn't have reached half the size.

We left our pushbikes by the fountain and helped each other over the fence and into the back garden. 'Do you know who lives here?' Cuba asked. I shook my head. 'Dey must be up doe, init?'

'Must be.'

My mama used to bring me to this house when I wasn't much older than a toddler. We wouldn't come inside – she wasn't as brazen as Cuba and me – we would only drive to the gate, and she would point up at the windows and tell me how she would imagine herself looking out of them when she was but a child herself.

She would cycle into Clifton and across the Suspension Bridge just to look at the yard. There were other houses on the road, for it was narrow with many mansions, but it was this one that caught her eye. It was the furthest from the street, she explained, as far from the hustle and bustle as one could get.

'You know man's gonna live here someday, cuz,' I announced. Cuba screwed his face; he didn't mean to doubt me, but he wasn't accustomed to dreams. 'How you gonna buy dis yard, akh? You need white people ps to buy dis – big man ting.' 'Don't watch dat,' I told him. 'Man'll find a way, truss me.'

Cuba put his arms across his little chest and huffed in the manner of a man about to embark upon yet another noble quest. 'Say no more, g, but if you're gonna buy it den man'll help you, init. Dat's what family's for.'

In the back garden the sun caught in the shade and couldn't strike the grass, but its efforts were rewarded with a mellow air that had paid no mind to the weather elsewhere. The grounds were vast, with streams that led from pond to pond, fruit trees and countless flowering shrubs.

'You know deh's horses in the woods, init?' I said, repeating what my mama had told me all those years ago.

'Horses?'

'Yeah, fam. White horses. And my marge told man dat Jesus rides on white horses, blud.'

'I bet dey would sell for ps den, init?' Cuba muttered. We fell silent as we thought about how many packets of sweets we could buy for a white horse that even Jesus would ride. 'You reckon we could sell dem?' he whispered.

I shrugged, and climbed into the low branches of a tree close to a pond. Cuba picked fallen twigs from the base and threw them as far as he could; they broke the surface of the water and floated idly. 'Only if you can catch dem first.' We looked at each other, the fire in our eyes ablaze like jasper stones, then we raced to the bottom of the garden and through the cast-iron gate at its foot.

We spent the entire afternoon chasing the shadows of those white horses, but we didn't catch the swish of a tail, nor the print of a hoof. We returned to the house-atop-the-hill downcast and defeated. I found my place in the tree again, and Cuba took up the twigs.

The water that ran from pond to pond had no foul smell. It was lazy, like a river of clarified honey. I thought if I knelt to taste it I might have refreshed myself after such a disappointing day, but Cuba had other ideas. He pointed towards the house. 'Yo, you wanna see what's inside?'

'How?' I asked.

He took a large stone from a rockery beside the pond and tossed it through the basement window. 'Watch what you're doing, blud!' I yelled. 'Don't break man's yard!'

Ready to run, we waited on tenterhooks for the sound of an alarm, but none came. 'Dis shit's so old,' Cuba said after a minute, 'man knew it wouldn't even have no security, fam.'

'What about my window, blud? Why'd you do dat?'

'Dey'll fix it before you buy it, g, don't worry,' Cuba grinned, 'and if dey don't, I'll send you some ps to cover it. It's calm, bro. We're in dis together, remember? Come, fam.' He swept the broken slivers from the window with his sleeve and we wriggled through a slit wide enough only for ten-year-old boys.

Inside were high ceilings, grand fireplaces, reception halls and drawing rooms. Whoever the owners were, they had spared no expense. Marble floors like sheets of glass. Huge chandeliers in each room. Cushions and carpets from countries outside of any I knew. The kitchen was stocked with an astonishing array of meats, a thousand jars containing every delicacy from marmalades to capers, an assortment of breads and cheeses, a cupboard full of sweet stuffs and an oven bigger than both of us.

And the bedrooms: they could have slept a hundred refugees. It was the first time I saw a pantry and a laundry room. The first time I'd travelled up four flights of stairs not in a block of flats. And that day I realised, more than ever, why my mama had fallen in love with the place; it was perfect – the perfect home. 'What do you reckon dese man do to afford all dis, cuz?' Cuba asked. 'You reckon dey shot?' He appeared in the doorway behind me with two watches hanging from his arm. He'd had to push them up to his elbow to keep them in place. Cuba handed me one as I handed him some food from a cupboard.

The watch was gold like the sofas in the living room and had four faces that ticked at different speeds and pointed to different measures of time. I pocketed it because finders keepers and losers weepers.

We spent the evening exploring the house, eating from the fridge and napping on the beds. We lived like kings until the day grew old and voices came from outside, adult voices. Cuba gripped my arm and we crept to the front door.

Outside, grown-ups were pointing at the house and a fed was crouched over the bikes. The adults told the officer that they were good friends with the owners, who were weekending, and that they had heard a crash out back and nothing since.

Cuba's grip tightened. 'Yo, we need to cut, g,' he whispered. We bolted back through the broken window and lost the law in the woods.

From there we ran home, back to Ends. And a decade passed until I reached my twentieth year.

To everything there may have been a season, but some things remained unchanged and I wouldn't rest until I owned that house-atop-the-hill.

2

> Enter by the narrow gate; for wide is the gate and broad is the way that leads to destruction, and there are many who go in by it. Because narrow is the gate and difficult is the way which leads to life, and there are few who find it. – Matthew 7:13–14

There are roads in neighbourhoods like mine all across the country. Broad roads. Without mansions. In England they have names like City Road or High Street, except this road was called Stapleton, and those familiar with her charm might call her Stapes. They were broad roads because they tracked their way from one side of Ends to the other. Ends was what we called our neighbourhood, or any neighbourhood like ours. I wasn't sure of the reason, whether it was because it was where the downtrodden saw the light at the end of the tunnel, or because once you arrived you only left when those in charge wanted to rebrand. Either way, it was stuffed to the gunwales with people trying to make ends meet, so the name made sense. It was a far cry from Clifton.

The moment you left the city's centre you could hear or smell Ends, whether you took a left after Stapes, or carried straight through Old Market. The sounds were disorderly. It smelt non-white. It was the other side of Abbey Road and industrial waste bins that were padlocked in other neighbourhoods hung and stank like open stomachs. You could find a million dreams deferred in the torn slips that littered outside the bookie's.

I loved and hated this road.

It would always have a place in my heart, a certain fondness I kept in acknowledgement of how it had shaped the man I had become. I had grown to know Shona right here too, and for that I was truly grateful. Still, I hated it because there was nowhere I was better known, a fact I would soon come to find more troublesome than I'd ever imagined. And nowhere was there a greater example of how much pain we could normalise as human beings.

The road was patrolled by young and old: abtis arranged tables outside cafes, serving tea from pans; they peered into the faces of young hijabis, trying to find a likeness and match daughter to hooyo. Their sons and nephews stood outside corner shops and met at park benches, and together with my cousins, they were watched by the disapproving eyes of our respective elders.

I belonged to the Hughes family. The infamous Hughes family – known to police and hospital staff across the city. Except in truth, I was a Stewart. It was the name written on my birth certificate, and it was my papa's name, but I owed it no allegiance.

Usually, the women in the Hughes family kept their surname if they ever married – which they did, several times – but my mama, Erica, had been all too quick to rid herself of such a burden. That was how my mama viewed any attachment to her maiden name. She twisted the familial bottle cap and poured past relationships down the drain like a wino intent on betterment. She had tried to impart her ideology on to me, but I was Hughes through and through.

A long time ago she had forsaken her desire for the house-atop-the-hill and, as a teen, had wed my papa, then a trainee pastor. And now, much to the mockery of our family, she was a pastor's wife and worship leader and had inherited two names instead of one. Like new shoes, Sister replaced Mrs, and Stewart ousted Hughes.

I had more cousins than rivers had rivulets, and like a doting stepmother, Stapes took us all in. A few of my aunties had council houses on the offshoots, and I think I had a cousin or two in the high-rises that overlooked the toings and froings of the busy road. Those who didn't live nearby could be found on Stapes more often than in their own homes – at Nanny's, in Ladbrokes or one of the yard shops, buying cassava and plantain. My likkle cousins might be found at the blue cage playing ball, and the elders might be at one of the free houses tossing dominoes and talking about things they knew nutun about.

My cousin Winnie called the street itself home. She slept on the Baptist church steps and begged cigarette stubs from the gutter. She said she found the gutter more giving than the people passing, but maybe the people passing had nutun left to give.

I sailed the pavements in June as one accustomed to the breaks in the concrete. I swayed clear of batty-man poles and touched fists with those who knew me well enough to acknowledge me, but not enough to ask how I was. And even if they had asked, I would've lied and said all was well.

My cousin Bunny spotted me from across the street and touched his hand to his heart, then to the sky. I returned his salute and we kept it pushing.

Bunny was a funny one, unpredictable like the weather. If there was a child in Ends without a father, we said it was Bunny's yute. He was to women what Vybz was to Jamaica's youth – at least that's what he thought.

He called himself the Garfield Sobers of infidelity.

Once, not long before my twentieth summer began, I had seen him sprawled across a bus stop, hair half cornrowed, tracksuit at his knees, with Winnie asleep on his thigh and a crack pipe in his hand. He'd looked at me through glass eyes but I didn't tarry. The next morning I saw him at the helm of an empty pram, walking through Cabot Circus in a cheap suit with two of his yutes on either side. His arm was linked with a young woman's who wasn't either of their mamas, and he held a brick phone to his ear with his shoulder.

I didn't take more than ten steps before bumping into my next relation. Sidestepping a shrivelled Kurd who shuffled with his head down and his hands held behind his back, I encountered the wide bosom of Aunty Paulette.

Aunty Paulette was my mama's younger sister and she had spent much of her life inside. She wore a fistful of gold rings and one of them chains from Claire's with the letter 'P' in bold italics. Her favourite thing to do was to jam her finger into older men's chests and tell them that she was twice the man they were.

'Wahum, Sayon,' she said, busy picking sup'm from her teeth with her tongue. 'Stand up straight wen mi ahh chat to yuh nuh man, yuh shoulders deh slouch an yuh look miserable, yuh just ahh ruin di day energy man, chuhh. Yuh see Bunny? Mi affi chat to im.'

I told her where I'd seen him. 'Who im deh wid?'

I told her he was alone.

'Good. Mi av ahh bone fi pick wid im, enuh.' She then proceeded to pick the bone with me. Apparently Bunny had borrowed a twenty sheet from her last week and was refusing to pay her back. Aunty Paulette had been forced to borrow the money from Nanny and now Nanny was at her neck because she couldn't play her numbers.

I struggled to appear concerned. I had some change on me, a little less than a grand – my aunty knew that – why else would she complain to her nephew? I took a ball of money from my pocket and unwound the elastic bands keeping the notes together. The house fund wouldn't miss it, so I gave her two twenties and suffered the kiss she planted on my cheek.

'Tenk yuh, Nephew,' she drawled, tucking the money into her brassiere and pushing the words over and around the mint in her mouth. 'Yuh keep outtah trouble now, yuh ear?' And just like that, Aunty Paulette was gone. Gone to inflict an earful upon the next man that eyed her the wrong way or looked at her rear a little longer than she liked.

The end of a dual carriageway split Stapes in two. If the first part was mini-Mogadishu or bantam-Hargeisa, the second (top side) was likkle Kingston: more bookies, barbers and chicken shops, more billboards and men sat low in coupés with dark windows.

There was a Pakistani-owned wig shop selling Brazilian hair to West African women. Across the street, their ill-mannered Caribbean competition saw less custom. Further up the road, on the corner of a branching avenue, blue-and-white police tape cordoned off the footpath where I'd taken Cordell's life not two days ago.

The difference between where I lived and where I wanted to be living was laughable. I wrung my hands as I walked and comforted myself with the knowledge that I would be rid of the filth soon; all I had to do was remain free.

The attending officers who were standing beside the tape scanned the crowds, looking for admissions of guilt in the dark faces of passing strangers, but I made it impossible for them, or anyone else watching, to read my trepidation. As ever, there was bop in my stride and a bounce to my gait, but my mind was split, contorted in a million directions, few of them fruitful. I'd worked hard these past years, and my boyhood dream was well within sight. If all went to plan, I would be able to offer the homeowners eighty per cent of the house's last valuation. Eighty per cent. Cash. By the end of the year. And with the promise of more to come – surely they couldn't refuse that? But it was just that which bothered me: *if all went to plan*. Because it was only June, and Cordell's death had me scrambling.

I checked the time. I had an appointment to keep and would be late if I dawdled, but as I approached the crime scene I felt I needed something to ease my spirit; and good company, even brief, could do that.

On any other day I would have crossed the carriageway and stopped at the first corner shop for a patty and a bag juice, so in order to maintain the appearance of normalcy that's exactly what I did.

The shopfront was painted a deep green and in a high, bright yellow scrawl the sign read: VIV'S.

Viv was an old-timer in Ends. He had come to England with the first ships in the late forties, moved to Bristol for dock work and sekkled a community. Viv's was open from March through October, when he packed up and went back ahh yard fi winter. 'Back to di wife,' he would always say. I would ask, 'Which one?' And he would wink and put a finger to his lips: 'Whichever one nuh baddah mi, star.'

His family was the only one older than mine in the city. We knew each other well and demonstrated our respect through patronage. I gave him an extra tenner each visit and dropped a couple of pounds in the charity box I knew he took a cut from.

Going home wasn't cheap; I didn't blame him.

As I entered the shop I shouted his name, but I needn't have bothered because the tinkle announced my entrance too. 'Viv,' I called. No answer. 'Yo, Viv, yuh cyaan ear mi?' I checked to make sure the officers hadn't followed me inside, then dropped loose change in a box claiming the money went to starving Africans and leant across the counter.

Through a hatch behind the till, a small set of stairs led to a basement that ran beneath two properties. It was where Viv kept his 'hexpensive liquors and hexcess stock'. It was also where he grew marijuana plants in a locked room. He hung the key around his neck next to a beaded chain and a rusted locket with a busted case. The exposed photograph in the locket was of him as a boy sat on his mama's knee. He wore a white frock to match his mama's sweeping hat and gown. Age had stained the picture pink, forcing rose-tinted spectacles on any who caught the young boy's eye.

I assumed the old man was with the greenery and that he wouldn't be long, so I tended the shop to pass the time. It would do well to take my mind from things.

Whilst I waited, two likkle yutes hustled into the store. They wore backpacks bigger than themselves and talked about footballing events from before they were born. They didn't give me a second glance. When I was coming up, an older would have checked us for that. A nod of deference was required, at the very least. I had thought it stupid then, but I understood it now. It was about respect. It was the acknowledgement of something bigger than ourselves. Still, the two yutes were in a world of their own, so I left them to it.

I propped the door ajar and stood in its entrance. In the middle of the road a dread was slowing both sides of the traffic as he shouted sweet nothings at a larger-than-life white woman across the street.

A mother took advantage of the temporary tailback and shooed her train of children between the cars. And behind the police tape I could make out the discoloured pavement where Cordell's blood had dried.

Two officers stood beside the tape ready to hurry any gawkers along, but since this wasn't Clifton, the scene was hardly worth much more than a passing glance.

I had never entered the adolescent stage of thinking myself immortal. My mortality was as real to me as the soil I shovelled onto the aunts, uncles and cousins we buried. That was one of the downfalls of having a large family: the funerals outnumbered even the weddings.

A reedy voice came from behind me: 'Yo, scuse me.' The two yutes were waiting to leave. The boy who spoke looked at me through hooded eyes, unsure of what resistance I would provide. The other yute hung at his arm and glared, but didn't offer a word.

'Unuh ain't buy nutun?' I asked. They shared a look.

'Nah,' the spokesman said. They each had their hands stuffed into their pockets, which were fuller than they had been when they arrived. I took my eyes from them and noticed the absence of a handful of sweets and chocolate bars from the counter.

'Say no more,' I nodded, opening the door for them to leave.

As they stepped on to Stapes and shared a triumphant smile, I recalled how close my ear had been to the streets at that age. 'Yo,' I called after them, they half turned, half made ready to run, but I beckoned them closer. 'You man heard what happened?' I asked, nodding towards the police tape. They followed my eye and shrugged. The spokesman reached for a Snickers, tore the wrapper and took a bite.

'I heard it was one Mali yute dat did it,' he said, but his friend was quick to disagree. He ripped a Skittles packet wide open and tipped some into his mouth.

'Nah, I heard it was one ahh dem man from Pauls.' They shrugged in unison again.

'Could've been anyone, init?' I replied, gladdened that the streets hadn't attached my cousin's name or mine to the hearsay. 'Aight, say

no more, enjoy the rest of your day you man; look after yourselves.'
They nodded and began to leave. 'An stop teefin,' I called after them.
They laughed and skipped away, revelling in the adrenaline rush that
being caught allowed.

It was all fun and games in the mind of a child. Consequences
were butts of reefers to be flicked into the road and any interference
was worthy of prejudice and scorn. But even in my youth I was far
removed from a child, and after what had happened, consequences
waited for me around the corner like chancers ready to pounce.

It didn't seem like Viv was coming back any time soon, so I paid
for the boys' sweets and sought a moment's comfort elsewhere.

3

If someone says, 'I love God,' and hates his brother,
he is a liar; for he who does not love his brother
whom he has seen, how can he love God whom he
has not seen? – 1 John 4:20

St Barnabas Baptist Church was the largest building on Stapleton
Road. It towered two storeys above Viv's, and its spires climbed
higher still. It was built during a time where the regulars would have
covered their noses with handkerchiefs and politely moved from the
pews where the current attendees sat.

Now it watched over the punters, trappers, drug abusers and
mentally ill with the silent disapproval of a wayward father re-entering
his child's life and finding an adult far from whom he had imagined
his child would become. In his children he had foreseen godly men.
Men of the good book. Oh, what disappointments they had become:
hypocrites and backsliders.

I found Winnie on the steps.

'Yo cuzzy,' she shouted, quickly moving to block my path. She
wore jeans that stopped way shy of her ankles and hips, and a brown

faux leather jacket with the sleeves rolled to the elbows. Her lips were cracked and her hair stiff like parched wool. 'You got anythink for me fam anythink at all money or food I don't mind I seent your girl's dad a minute ago.'

'Is he inside?'

'Nah he just left in a hurry looking like that man that carries the world on his back what's his face some Greek mythology person Antman or sup'm I don't know I seent your girl and her mum last week too Shona's real real pretty pretty like an angel she is ain't she I think that every time I seen her enuh?'

'Did her pops say anyting to you?'

'Nah nah he didn't say nothink to me but he gave me these.' She showed me her palm. He'd given her five pounds in silvers, so I added another five.

'You sure my man didn't say nutun?' I asked again. It was always best to check twice with Winnie. 'Didn't mention he was meetin man? What it was about or nutun?'

'Yeah yeah I'm sure Sayon man I told you I'm sure he ain't say nothink.'

'Say nutun. What you sayin, you ate today?'

'Nah nah you know sometimes I forget init.' She shifted on the balls of her feet and repeatedly re-counted her change. She rarely paused for breath. 'Just been busy you know praying talking to God making sure He know I'm all right cos you know Jesus cares about us init you me Midnight Hakim Shona's parents Erica your daddy Nanny and the rest of our family too Killa Calvin we're sinners all sinners you know but Jesus washed Jesus washed and washed our sins away you know dat init yeah you know that her dad let me inside his church the other day enuh?

'Yeah, I seent him the other day and he axed me to help him move a couple chairs and gave me some food real food not your food that wouldn't make any sense if Pastor gave me dat kind of food den he'd go to Hell not Heaven and dat wouldn't make any sense cos dem guys done the place up nice since I last seent it init lick of paint does wonders init?'

I might have asked Winnie if she'd heard anything about Cordell – after all, bitties were the biggest gossips – but I didn't want to keep the pastor waiting. If I didn't leave, I would end up taking her across the city to collect God knows what from God knows who. I gave her the little food I had left and cut.

Like my papa, Shona's papa was a pastor. The pastor of the Baptist church whose steps Winnie called home. And the pastor of the church whose eyes fell hot on my back as I travelled further and further down the road.

The right honourable Pastor Lyle Jennings.

A car sped past, almost hitting the kerb, and it drew me from the intimacy of my thoughts. It didn't slow, but I glimpsed my cousin Cuba in the passenger seat. He saw me too and stuck his head from the window with a grin, signalling that they'd spin back in a second. I waved and crossed the street as the whip disappeared as quickly as it had come.

Cousins were raised as siblings in the Hughes family.

As the oldest living family member, Nanny was the matriarch and everyone did as she said. She bickered with the men in the yard and seasoned food with the women. And she told us to get along, so we did.

That was how Aunty Paulette's second son, Cuba, became my brother.

Cuba and I were born a few months apart. I was in the year above at school, but age ain't nutun but a number and neither of us cared. He was wise beyond his years. We were like twins, though I was red and he was black like treated sugar beets. The rest of our cousins were either red like me or lighter-skinned and they used to mock his blackness sup'm fierce; they called him A-Quarter-Past-Midnight, Midnight and The-Dead-of-Night. Nanny too. Cuba was dark like her papa and that didn't sit well in her spirit, but since it got under his skin I never joined them.

Both Cuba and I were around the six-foot mark, with short hair that faded to skin. We could sleep for a matter of minutes and would never get bags under our eyes. Our skin was gloss, with or without lotion. We were smooth criminals and butter wouldn't melt in our mouths.

Every one of my cousins was raised at Nanny's and we all had spent varying degrees of time there as yutes, but none more so than Cuba and me. My parents were never much taken with this world, and by extension their only child. And when Aunty Paulette was free and sober enough to take care of Cuba, her unease with the responsibilities of motherhood made her beat him shades of blue like black boys in moonlight.

The closeness of our age and the vast amounts of time we had spent together were reflected in our kinship. We walked to school and back together. Ate and bathed together. We liked the same stories and sports teams, the same treats, and were drawn to the same people. We were close with the rest of our cousins, but that was always who they were to us: the rest.

When I was six and Cuba five, the two of us would make a game of climbing Winnie's back and racing through the house like Black cowboys at high noon.

One time, Winnie tripped and knocked Cuba's big brother Jamaal to the floor. Dazed, Jamaal reached for whatever his hand landed on and it landed on me. Whilst he mounted and begun beating me, Winnie took off upstairs and Cuba bolted for the kitchen. He came back with a knife and buried it in his brother's leg.

Even at that young age, riding Winnie's back, playing penny on the wall and pretending to be a grown-up, I knew that I could kill for him. After all, there was no one I loved more on Earth or in Heaven. Except I hadn't thought that my conviction would one day be tested, especially against someone I'd once considered a friend. ∎

OUR STRATFORD

The Herak Family

Introduction by Damian Le Bas

They carry the name of Heracles, and they live in Stratford, east London. The Herak family are Romani people, or Roma: not Romanians – which is an ethnonym derived from the ancient Romans – but Roma, a word with a Sanskrit root, and which can mean 'husbands', 'Romani people' or simply 'us'. Over the past thousand years the Roma have gone by whole directories of other names, some merely misnomers (Egyptians – whence 'Gypsies' – and Turks), and some, at least originally, blunt and vile (*Tsiggánoi, Çigany, Zigeuner*: all of which share the root meaning 'Untouchable Ones'). But if the name 'Roma' and, to whatever degree, those people who call themselves Roma, are of sometime Indian heritage, then why would such a family, ambling along a footbridge in twenty-first-century England, bear a Greek-derived name, when they aren't even from Greece?

There are many answers. Most Roma, whatever their far-flung ancestry, are Europeans going back tens of generations. And though there are still families, like my own, who have only lately begun to move off 'the road', large numbers of so-called Gypsies come from families who have not been nomadic for several hundreds of years.

They are often deeply rooted in the countries in which they live, sometimes with medieval provenance there.

The Heraks, for instance, hail in recent generations from Slovakia. They speak three languages at home: Slovak, English and a Slovak dialect of the Romani language. That is to say, three Indo-European languages, of which Romani is the most recent arrival in Europe, thoroughly influenced by centuries of life here and, prior to that, in the Caucasus and Persia. Then there is the land of the divine hero Heracles: Greece itself – specifically, the Byzantine Empire into which the Roma arrived, their forebears having set out westward from India around the year AD 1000. Greece became one of the crucibles of an evolving Romani culture, a sort of second motherland. As a result, the Romani language is strewn with Greek words – alongside Armenian and Persian ones. Scholars like to call them 'lexical items' and 'borrowings', as if they were physical, or somehow in short supply: as if, by taking them on their journey, the Roma had left their original owners bereft. This traffic in vocabulary worked in both directions, though, and Romani words from India have been left behind wherever the Roma have lived, from Tehran to Helsinki.

Britain has a long-established Romani presence, stretching back to a probable first arrival in late-fifteenth-century Scotland: many of the country's Traveller families are descended from these early migrations. In addition, there are perhaps as many as 200,000 Romani people in the UK whose families moved here in recent decades from continental Europe. Few take after the popular image of Gypsies. Almost all recent Romani immigrants, like the Heraks, live in brick-and-mortar housing, and are quietly getting on with regular jobs and uncontroversial lifestyles. If anything makes them stand out, it might be their appreciation of the fact that, in British schools, Roma children aren't put into separate teaching groups for children with less potential. In 2015 the European Commission initiated proceedings against Slovakia because of this practice, apparently with little effect. Five years later, in 2020, the Ministry of Education of the Slovak Republic wrote to the Commission acknowledging the continued existence of racially segregated education, while quibbling over how it should be defined, and UNESCO's Global Education Monitoring team have found that, as of this year, the country's Romani children are still frequently taught in classes apart, with few chances to shine.

In Romani families' photographs there always seem to be signals of a taste for the resplendent. The Heraks' photographs are no different. Few companies set out to make things with Romani buyers in mind, so a 'Gypsy look' has to be mustered from whatever goods are available: English Romani Travellers call this look 'a kushti turnout' or 'a bit of flash': continental Roma might mention a 'shukar kher', a beautiful home. Individually, these objects could be anyone's – an assortment of gilded frames, an Italian-style dining table with matching white-and-gold upholstered chairs, and vases and goblets, most of them glitzy and golden to some degree, all of it viewed through gold-framed sunglasses with cinnamon-tinted lenses – but collectively, this assemblage of choices seems to call out 'Roma' to me. So many Romani homes contain these notes of a gilded, Mediterranean-inflected interior design. They are indicative not so much of nomadism, or a hankering after a particular 'old country', as they might be seen in a southern European expat's home. More so, they speak of a simple desire for little flecks of domestic glamour: small touches of luxury. A detached rural pile, a London flat, a trailer on a tarmacked suburban camp: any of these can have a Romani visual tang. In places, each of them has. Even within one family – mine, for instance – there are examples of all these kinds of abode. The Roma understand that a home doesn't need axles and wheels to be 'Gypsy', and we look for other signs.

In the 1970s, the English Romani Traveller Clifford Lee joined a *National Geographic* road trip that traced, in reverse, the Romani migration from Rajasthan to Britain (back then, it was still feasible to undertake such a journey by car). Lee was often moved by the resemblances he noticed between his own relations and the Gypsies he met on the long road from France to Afghanistan and beyond. Looking at the Herak family's photographs, I have a curious parallel feeling: of prying through someone else's family album, but also discovering that it is – however delicately – connected to my own. I experience that fragile but stirring sense of familiarity that Gypsies often speak of, as Lee did – to notice in a stranger the line of a cousin's jaw, the shade of an aunt's heavy glance, a stoical fatherly gaze, or a baby's gurgle of mirth, her head adorned with a soft pink bow.

Like all people, though, we are just as prone to being connected by things that have little to do with our descent. Like me, the Heraks are interested in English history, and they spend their spare time visiting palaces and castles, reading books and painting. Like my parents, Valentina Herak and her father practice tai chi.

Often caricatured as a society of chaos, theft, and even of frivolous violence, Romani culture behind closed doors is a civilisation of nuzzles and cuddles, of constant pecks on the cheek. I sense those habits – the ones I grew up among – in the Heraks' pictures: of parents, big sisters and uncles who dole out generous, laughing hugs, and of children accustomed to relatives scooping them up and squeezing them tight, peppering them with kisses. My relations' lives – particularly those of the ones who'd lived the 'old way', travelling with wagons, tents and horses – seemed to play out on a wider than average spectrum of tactility. On the one hand, they were often boxers, drilled in the thought that self-defence was a precondition of life. But for the most part, they were also great embracers, consolers, bearers of loving arms. In other words, exactly the sort of adjustable physicality that one might expect from people who'd dwelt on the margins, often disliked. They had to stand as bulwarks against that dislike, and be skilled in consoling each other when the defences were overrun.

Conjoined as we are by language, by culture and sometimes by physical resemblance, Romani people are connected just as powerfully by Europe's blunders, hexes and mistakes: by cultural errata. A thousand years' worth of accreted misunderstandings shapes our present. The result is a patina of mystery, howbeit its ingredients are not especially mysterious: a mixture of group blaming, superstitions and etymological false friends. The popular tale of the Gypsies is gaffe-strewn, lacking consistency, but vigorous and often bursting with wild-eyed certainty. This received thought-picture is deeply etched on Europe's subconscious, and maybe permanently so. It is a painting that has come down through the family and one that Europe, having inherited it, has a limited urge to part with.

There are false trails in these pictures, too. I saw the brick-red sarcophagi of Calor-branded gas bottles, explosive amphorae that might symbolise off-grid capabilities, or simply a lack of access to more convenient, less combustible forms of power, and was reminded of my family's yard full of trailers, each one with such a gas bottle stationed outside. But then I realised this is simply a picture of a narrowboat on the Regent's Canal: the nomad in me on high alert for what turns out to be waterborne – and likely non-Romani – nomadism. It made me smirk at my own assumptions: the prejudices of a Gypsy regarding Gypsies.

I wonder, if you were to look at these pictures alone, with no writing accompanying them, whether you would see anything more than snapshots of a normal, happy family. A walk alongside the canal; a resting stop in a garden; smiling at babies; holding the young ones' hands as they cross the road. The souls that give a city of glass and viaducts its meaning. In one way, that is all I see, and perhaps that is as it should be. ■

EDITOR'S NOTE: The photographs in 'Our Stratford' were taken by the Herak family using disposable cameras. *Granta*'s photography editor, Max Ferguson, met the family in their home and together they spent the day walking around Stratford. With sincere thanks to the Herak family and Szymon Glowacki, Stronger Communities Outreach Lead at Protection Approaches, for making this project possible. See more at protectionapproaches.org

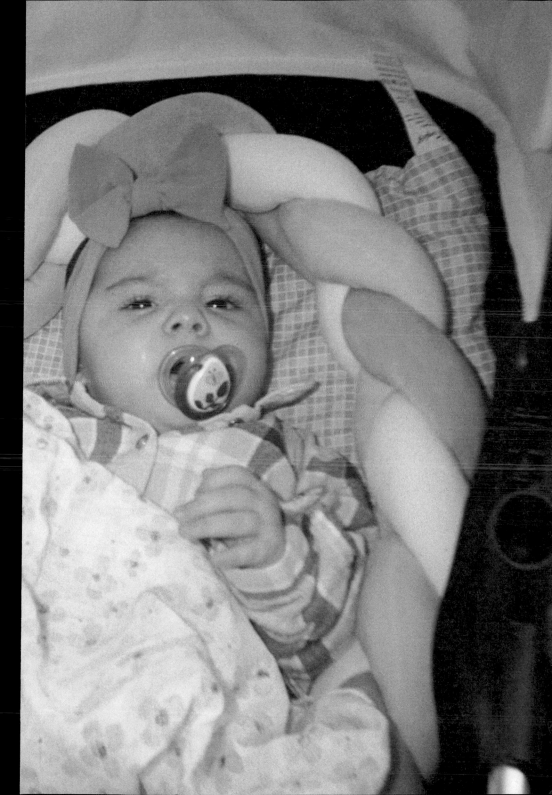

P A | Protection Approaches

From hate crime to online extremism, from structural discrimination to mass atrocities, identity-based violence has become an all-too-common fact of daily life. Hate movements, armed groups, and governments are exploiting identity to divide us, manipulating our differences in the pursuit of power, a particular political agenda, or an exclusionary ideology.

As Covid-19's economic and political consequences deepen, climate-driven crises become more common, and populist authoritarian movements threaten to upend long-standing democratic rule, identity-based violence, including mass atrocities, will become more frequent, systematic, and entrenched.

Protection Approaches exists to meet these challenges head-on.

From our local programmes in communities and schools to our global efforts to confront mass atrocities and genocide, we are working to build a world where everyone accepts and respects each other, regardless of identity. We believe that this mission is not only possible but probable, and are dedicated to doing the long-term, difficult work necessary to help make it a reality.

Our team are working right now to support LGBTQI+ communities facing atrocities in Afghanistan, East and South East Asian communities facing hate crime in the UK, and Roma communities facing persecution across Europe.

With your help, we can turn the rising tide of identity-based violence and build a world free from prejudice, hate, and inequality.

To find out more about what we do and to donate please visit: **protectionapproaches.org**

Stella Urbanski (right) and her daughter Mary Urbanski, 1969
Courtesy of the author

THE PICNIC PAVILION

Debbie Urbanski

Monday

After my first surgery but before my second, I sit with my dead grandmothers and my dead aunt at the county park under the picnic pavilion. The sun is going down, and a breeze blows in from the north and ripples the polluted lake water in front of us.

The lake is vast and there is an asphalt walking trail around its shores, and a dock, oaks, views.

We sit formally on the edge of the benches of the brown picnic table, feet pressed to the ground, spines straight, hands in our laps. How people would sit among strangers, which in most ways we are, having not seen each other for a decade or decades in some cases.

My dead grandmothers are wearing day dresses in ornate floral prints. My dead aunt is also wearing a dress though hers is a solid color with puffed sleeves and neckline detailing.

I know about the styles of their dresses because I looked up on the internet what women like my dead grandmothers or my dead aunt wore when leaving the house in the 1950s or 1970s respectively.

They are the age they were when they died: sixty-one, fifty-eight, fifty-nine. They are also barefoot. I don't know what happened to their shoes.

Surely they were buried or, in my aunt's case, cremated while wearing shoes.

One of the differences between my three dead relatives and me is that they are not wearing shoes. Another difference is they are translucent, meaning if I look through them I can see the complicated surface of the lake. Translucent ghosts are somewhat of a cliché; I wish they weren't. They are wearing dresses. I am not wearing a dress. Another difference is they're dead and I am not dead.

Perhaps it would be more interesting to focus on our similarities.

None of us have our uteruses anymore.

None of us have our ovaries, fallopian tubes or cervixes.

Lately I have been around a lot of women who still possess their fertility, their quickened metabolisms, their natural estrogen, their vaginal lubrication and their eggs. I am tired of being around such women.

Three of us, my dead grandma Stella, my dead aunt Mary and myself, share the pathogenic variant c.4035delA of the BRCA1 gene. This variant, the cause of their gynecological cancers, killed them. If I follow none of the National Comprehensive Cancer Network's management recommendations for what is known as Hereditary Breast and Ovarian Cancer syndrome, chances are I will get cancer, and perhaps that cancer will also kill me.

My dead grandmother Helen, on my mother's side, does not share this variant; she had unlucky ovaries.

Though one might argue we are all unlucky.

One might also argue that my three dead relatives are unlucky while I, with my fancy-pants DNA testing and prophylactic surgeries, am lucky and haunted.

So here we are, lucky, unlucky, haunted, all of us in menopause, me a few months in, they for decades.

If dead women are still in menopause.

'Yes we are still indeed in menopause,' clarifies my dead grandma Stella, baring her teeth, which appear for a moment to be sharpened.

I thank them for coming, comparing one's family to a compass.

'Like I had a choice,' says my dead grandma Stella.

'Like you had other things to do,' says my dead aunt Mary.

My dead grandma Helen questions whether this conversation need happen at this particular part of the day when the sun is going down and the dark arriving. Why not chat at sunrise or the following high noon?

'To avoid the inevitable clichés,' she advises.

I don't think she would have used a phrase like *the inevitable clichés* when she was alive.

My dead grandma Stella laughs and says not to worry. She says, motioning to me, 'This is already one big cliché.' The gilded child with a destiny summoning forth, from a place of guilt, privilege and safety, her ghostly ancestors, to ask for counsel and closure –

But she is wrong about my motivation.

'I'm not a child,' I insist.

Unless my lack of reproductive organs has made me childlike.

Though even little girls have uteruses.

I want to discuss what my dead relatives and I have in common.

When I lift my shirt, scars ring my abdomen like little pink hyphens.

'Oh they removed much more than that in my debulking!' chuckles my dead grandma Helen, who, in addition to losing her ovaries, fallopian tubes, cervix and uterus, also lost parts of her colon, and small intestine, and the layer of fatty tissue known as the omentum that once wrapped around her abdominal organs. She lifts her dress.

Her scar, much larger than mine, rises vertically from her pubic bones up around her navel.

'My first surgery felt like I was in the hospital and I was never going home. My second surgery felt like doctors cut a hole in my trachea, inserted a plastic endotracheal tube and connected me to a ventilator,' she says.

After my grandma's second surgery, she couldn't talk. Instead of talking, she wrote on a pad of paper. She wrote, *a shot for pain.* She wrote, *I WANT.* Seven weeks later she died from acute gastrointestinal bleeding due to or as a consequence of erosive gastritis due to or as a consequence of cancer of the ovaries with other significant conditions of liver and pulmonary failure.

My own doctors should not cut a hole in my throat for my second surgery, she assures me.

'My God, Helen, pull your dress down already!' chides my dead grandma Stella.

I unpack the hot-water carafe and the cups and saucers and metal infusers from the willow picnic basket I brought from home and brew four cups of a honey-bush peppermint blend.

'The funny thing is,' I say, 'for so many years, I wanted to die. Depression and so on. But you were the ones who died. Then here I am, trying very hard not to die!'

'That's not really funny,' says my dead grandmother Stella.

My dead relatives sip their tea.

I can only get little glimpses of them, like they're in the corner of the camera frame, flashing in and out of the frame.

I have been wondering what will happen to my breasts when, a week from today, they are removed from my body.

Do breasts get incinerated? Or thrown into the garbage? Or into a burial pit, or compost bin –

I would rather my breasts not be reduced to garbage and ash.

Perhaps, after the pathology tests, they'll allow me take the tissue home.

'Do you think the doctors will ask me if I want to take my breast tissue home?' I ask.

My dead aunt says, 'No. I don't think they'll ask you that.'

I tell them, 'After my first surgery, my left leg went numb. My gynecological oncologist surgeon said yes, that does happen. Things are so close together down there, she said. Sometimes the nerve will come back or sometimes not. I miss feeling the upper part of my leg.'

A man in a wooden boat rows away from the shore. He is rowing west toward another shore. Above him the sky balances between darkness and light. This isn't the type of lake one would swim in due to the industrial pollution, particularly the heavy metals. But the water in such light – in such darkness? – looks golden or honeyed as the sun flashes light as it –

My dead grandmother Stella interrupts. 'Please do not say that we are watching the sun sink below the horizon. Do not say the sun disappears in a wash of color. Do not talk about the sun's serious reflection in the water or the fading sun's light in the clouds. Please, do not mention the sun again today. We've had more than enough melodrama for one day.'

Okay, I will not mention the sun.

The light is fading anyway.

'I always thought horror stories were supposed to be scary,' I say. 'Horror?'

I motion to them. 'Ghosts and so on.'

'Oh, honey. We're not what you should be afraid of.'

The weeks and months of their collective suffering condense around us causing the air to glisten, and for a little while it becomes hard to see the lake.

Tuesday

'This is the last Tuesday that I'll have breasts,' I tell my dead grandmothers and my dead aunt.

Again during sunset we are sitting at the picnic pavilion, the one with the vast lake views that is popular for weddings in the warmer months.

I had intended to arrive earlier in the day when the sun was in the center of the sky and radiating its life-giving yet destructive energy but my son had refused to do his chores, and my daughter disappeared from the house in a flood of prepubescent hormones.

I had to find my daughter and convince my son to put away his clothes.

Hence the lateness of my arrival.

My dead relatives have been waiting for me.

My dead aunt Mary says that she spent the time frightening the ducks.

They are wearing more casual dresses today, what my mom calls house dresses, even my dead aunt who is of a different generation.

House dresses generally weren't worn outside, to, say, a park.

There must be different rules when one is dead.

To identify the patterns of their dresses, I googled *1950s common house dresses patterns fabrics*: polka dots and fun checkered prints.

The water hits the rocks along the shore.

The water hits the rocks along the shore again.

On the way to the picnic pavilion I had stopped at an independent coffee shop to purchase four medium steamed milks flavored with vanilla syrup and topped with grated nutmeg, which I now set onto the weathered picnic table. Beside the cups I place Susan Gubar's *Memoir of a Debulked Woman: Enduring Ovarian Cancer*.

'Another one?' sighs my dead aunt Mary.

I have read many cancer books this year: *The Undying: A Meditation on Modern Illness*; *The Emperor of All Maladies: A Biography of Cancer*; *Previvors: Facing the Breast Cancer Gene and Making Life-Changing Decisions*; *Confronting Hereditary Breast and Ovarian Cancer: Identify Your Risk, Understand Your Options, Change Your Destiny*; and *The Breast Reconstruction Guidebook: Issues and Answers from Research to Recovery*. This most recent memoir, the memoir of a debulked woman, is the first to focus solely on ovarian cancer.

'The cancer that killed you,' I add knowingly, nodding toward my dead grandma Helen and my dead aunt Mary.

My grandma Stella died of uterine cancer, my guess is uterine papillary serous carcinoma, a particularly aggressive and deadly type more common in BRCA1 mutation carriers.

My dead aunt Mary asks why am I so interested all of a sudden in them and their cancers. 'Is it because you don't have your ovaries anymore? And you think women who don't have their ovaries are automatically connected?'

I haven't yet mentioned that I am writing an essay about them.

Or, rather, an essay about me, and they are in the essay.

Their role in this essay is to illuminate me and my year of surgeries.

It is a narcissistic essay but it has been a narcissistic year.

I explain, 'When author Susan Gubar was told she had advanced ovarian cancer and would likely die, she felt "a moment of extraordinary calm . . . a spontaneous and weird sense of liberation." How did you feel when you found out that you had cancer and that you were dying? Were you calm or extraordinarily calm?'

My dead grandma Helen sips from her insulated cup.

She crosses her legs above the knee and gazes across the lake, where the sun is descending toward the trees on the far shore. The lake water moves; this has always been a windy place.

She says, 'Oh my, you are prying.'

I had planned on taking notes so I write down what my dead grandmother said. I write down, *You are prying.*

In addition to how it feels to die of cancer, I am also trying to understand treatments for ovarian cancer and how those treatments felt.

Again, Susan Gubar: 'Current remedies do not cure the disease. Instead, they debilitate the person dealing with it until she barely recognizes her mind, spirit, or body as her own. Enduring ovarian cancer mires patients in treatments more patently hideous than the symptoms originally produced by the disease.'

I ask my dead relatives, 'Is that also how you felt? How much did your treatments hurt?'

My dead aunt Mary says, 'I was fifty-one at the time of my first diagnosis.' That is all she says.

These dead women are not giving me much to work with.

I write down what my dead aunt said, word for word, wanting to be accurate.

'Also,' I say, 'Gubar writes, "It is hard to find happily-ever-after stories about ovarian cancer; it is hard to read stories without happily-ever-after endings." Do you agree with that statement?'

'Are you going to quote us the entire book?' asks my dead grandma Stella. She tugs at the front of her dress lowering the hem, an efficient and modest motion using both her hands.

It is a gesture that a woman in a home movie I found on YouTube does with her hands.

In the evenings I have been watching old home movies on YouTube, other people's, backyard cookouts, birthday celebrations, women walking in and out of kitchens, holidays, dancing, to get specific ideas for character movement in this essay. Otherwise my dead grandmothers are just sitting there beside the picnic table and my dead aunt is just sitting there, out of focus, hazy.

'I don't think legally I'm allowed to quote the entire book,' I say. 'Still, I recommend you read it. There are some very lyrical and moving sections. For instance, after the author's formal diagnosis, she writes about telling her daughters, "I will love you beyond my death. I will love you from another space that you will palpably feel, and feel to be me loving you." Did you tell anyone that or do you want to tell me that now?'

My dead aunt Mary laughs. Not because anything is funny but because that is the only gesture of hers I can remember.

She stops laughing.

She used to own a sailboat. Once a year, she would invite my family to sail on her boat around Lake Michigan.

I try to remember how she moved around the deck of the boat but I can't remember.

I told my mom I remember my aunt Mary dressed in beiges and whites and she said no, no, your aunt wore black, although she decorated her house in neutrals.

I return to YouTube and watch, again, the home movies of strangers.

A woman from California stands in the sun beside a black car and brushes her hair using long efficient strokes.

My dead aunt Mary in the setting sun beside the polluted lake brushes her hair – I think it is her real hair – in the same fashion. She doesn't mind the mimicry.

'Oh, I mind, dear,' she says.

She wore a wig to my wedding.

One's real hair must return when one becomes a ghost.

My dead aunt Mary puts the brush away. 'I know – let's play a game!' she exclaims. The game is called What Does This Granddaughter (Or Niece) Want From Us.

'Some kind of wisdom?'

'Or wealth?'

'Or content?'

'Or direct quotes?'

'Or armor?'

'Or absolution?'

'Or a spell book?'

'Or a looking glass?'

The game ends when the sun sets.

The sun sets.

Later in the evening, my mom sends me some photographs of my dead relatives. The photographs were taken at different people's weddings, my mother's, my older sister's. In some of these pictures my dead relatives are younger than me. In others, they are around my age, and in these later pictures, their cancer must have already begun inside of them, a single damaged cell or a small group of damaged cells that no one is going to pay any attention to for years. My impulse is to describe the infancy of their cancers as a form of visible light gathered around their abdomens, something otherworldly and destructive smeared across the fronts of their dresses.

Wednesday

'This is the last Wednesday I'll have breasts,' I tell my dead relatives.

'Oh my God, are we going to do this every day?' asks my dead grandma Stella, rolling her eyes, her hair swept up in wide unmoving curls.

Once again we are sitting at the picnic pavilion beside the lake in the setting light of the sun, although today my dead grandmothers and my dead aunt are dressed for a wedding. Their outfits are from the photos my mom texted me the previous night.

My dead grandmothers are wearing their shiny mother-of-the-bride dresses, white corsages pinned above their hearts, above their breasts.

My dead aunt is in a scoop-neck sweater-dress and hoop earrings, what she wore to my sister's first wedding, glitter in her hair.

For a while they pose contentedly on the sheltered concrete slab, smiling and flickering.

My dead grandma Helen raises her hand into what's left of the day's light and shows us how the light shines through her hand. My mom said maybe later she could find some pictures of my dead relatives not taken at a wedding. I didn't feel like bringing refreshments to the picnic pavilion today.

That morning I had spent attempting to track down medical records for my dead grandmothers beginning with my dead grandma Stella, thinking such primary documents would help them appear more real to me and less flickering.

I spent most of that time on hold, pressing 1 or pressing 2.

In addition to my grandma Stella herself being dead, her husband is dead, her siblings are dead, and her two daughters (including my aunt Mary) are dead. Her doctor is also dead.

Eventually I learned my dead grandmother's medical records had been destroyed, more specifically they were burned, shredded, pulped or pulverized. This feels like an enormous and physical loss to me.

My dead grandma Stella offers sarcastic applause. 'I do love a wild goose chase,' she snickers.

I have noticed my dead relatives are sounding like me or at least a part of me, the part of me in frequent disagreement with myself and annoyed with my tendency toward dramatics and histrionics, the eager inner critic –

'And whose fault is that, dear? Whose sloppy characterization and imaginative shortcomings are we really talking about?'

I propose a different question: what if one of them were kind?

The kind relative could smooth my hair and tell me everything is going to be all right.

'She thinks everything is going to be all right!' cackles my dead grandma Helen. The others join in, laughing. When they stop laughing, my dead aunt volunteers. She had, after all, when alive, been a grade-school science teacher. From what I remember she had, in fact, been kind.

Her face softens as she reaches toward me to smooth my hair.

'Everything is going to be all right,' she tells me. Her touch feels like a change in temperature. When she removes her hand, I notice her fingernails are bleeding.

'I'm scared of pain,' I confess.

'You are a brave person,' she says, bleeding.

'I'm scared of the surgery as well,' I confess.

'I know you can do this,' she says.

'I feel like I'm putting words into your mouth,' I confess.

She nods in agreement, bleeding. 'You are making the right decision.'

My dead grandma Stella offers my dead aunt Mary a vintage handkerchief for her blood then asks me what size replacement breasts I plan to get during my reconstruction. I tell her I am not getting reconstructed, rather I am planning a chest tattoo after my flat-closure mastectomy scars heal. I am considering a tattoo of three migratory yet symbolic and ascending birds. The birds would represent my dead grandmothers and my dead aunt flying away from me. The birds could also represent my uterus, my breasts and my ovaries flying away from me.

I expect my dead relatives to be grateful for this proposed tribute and proud.

My dead grandma Stella isn't grateful or proud. She is angry. 'What about all your other dead relatives?' she asks. I didn't think so many birds would be as meaningful. 'Excuses,' she mutters, stomping her left foot significantly onto the damp September ground.

There is the illogical sound of shattering. The lake fills with dead women in patterned dresses.

My dead grandmother explains to me, as if I didn't know, that these dead women are the sixty-two generations of dead women who died of female cancers because of my family's pathogenic variant which has been traced back to fifth-century Lithuania.

'I know, Grandma,' I say.

The dead women's heads emerge from beneath the water, their hair writhing with silver fish, their fingernails silvery and cold like the insides of oyster shells, their crinolines swelling.

The geese in the lake squawk warnings. Boat motors stall.

The men in the boats panic as they drift away in an undulation of unbraided hair.

'You need to memorialize them all,' orders my dead grandma Stella. Or does she say *memorize*?

At first I think the dead women are swimming or at least treading in place.

The dead women can't swim. Their arms are flailing, the hems of their wet dresses clinging to their open mouths. The lake is sixty-three feet deep and swimming is not allowed.

I tell my dead grandmother to send them back. She accuses me of silencing or forgetting. 'If we don't send them back, what do we do with them?' I ask.

The dead women in the lake tilt back their heads as if they are studying the sky. They are not studying the sky, they are drowning. The silver fish are eating their toes.

I run toward the lake and kneel on a boulder near the shore.

'You will need thousands of birds on your body!' shouts my dead grandma Stella.

I promise to get thousands.

I'm lying. My body isn't large enough.

Nonetheless I extend my arm.

The dead women don't notice my arm.

They continue drowning.

They all drown, sinking below the water, their hair tangling in the currents.

I retch onto the tiny white clam shells that make up the shore.

I didn't know ghosts could drown.

'Of course we can drown,' scoffs my dead grandma Stella.

The lake is full of bodies and dresses; the wind blows our shadows long.

I trudge back to the picnic pavilion.

'See you tomorrow,' I say, leaving my dead aunt and my dead grandmothers behind me at the park. I do not want to drive home with ghosts in my car. So many of the stories that terrified me as a child begin with the ghost of an unfortunate woman in the passenger seat of a car.

'See you tomorrow,' echo my dead relatives.

Thursday

'You know what I remembered?' I ask my dead grandma Helen at the picnic pavilion beside the lake as the sun sets undramatically without color, more falling than setting today. 'You used to speak to me years ago when I was planning my wedding. You spoke to me in poetry! Here, I looked up one of the poems. What a weird coincidence. There you were, talking to me back then. And here you are, talking to me now!'

My dead grandmother Helen is still wearing her wedding outfit from the day before, they all are.

'So lazy,' my dead grandma mutters as she skims through my poem. The multitude of dead women's bodies are no longer visible in the water. This doesn't mean the women's bodies are no longer there; all it means is I can't see them right now.

'I don't believe that was me talking,' decides my dead grandmother Helen.

I tell her how some of the poems from this series, the series in which she talked to me, were published in well-respected literary journals. I share the names of the well-respected journals.

'Haven't heard of them,' she says.

'You weren't kind then either,' I say. 'In addition, I remembered last night that you were in another story of mine but I put us in South Dakota and you were haunting me again, only this time you were haunting me on the front porch of an antique store. You were giving me relationship advice. And how you always wore red, white and blue. You had a hole in your chest that exposed your heart.'

My dead grandma pulls aside the frail fabric of her dress. 'At least you got that detail correct,' she says. The hole leading to her heart is intimate and weepy and red.

'But I'm exploring the essay form now. I find it interesting how women writers are always quoting somebody else's text then interacting with the text to form the shape of their essay. I want to use that form here.'

'If you're trying to impress us, you're not impressing us,' says my dead grandmother Stella. She considers doing something scary with the shape of her body but decides against it.

'In another book about cancer called *The Undying*, Anne Boyer writes, "Women with cancer are often forced to watch themselves dissolve, lamentable objects intolerable as lamenting ones, witnesses to everyone else's sad stories but socially corrected as soon as a sadness issues from their own mouths."'

'I don't care,' says my dead grandma Stella.

'I'm wondering if I'm doing this to you, making you dissolve, again, and making you watch your dissolvement. And am I doing this for selfish reasons? I want to talk about my suffering but I don't want to talk about it alone.'

'Your suffering?' asks my dead grandma Helen, laughing softly to herself.

'Look, if you want to write non-fiction, can you just write non-fiction?' says my dead grandma Stella. 'Like how about a straightforward essay where you talk about your surgeries and your guilt in a series of narrative scenes that actually happened?'

'What I think my mom means,' explains my dead aunt Mary, 'is if you'd like to write about yourself, about what you're going through, or will go through, can you do that without all this –' She motions to herself, to the ghosts hovering on either side of her.

'But I want to hear what you have to say. That's the point of this exercise.'

'Oh she wants to hear what we have to say!'

One of my dead grandmothers opens her mouth and screams.

The thing about being a ghost and screaming is that the sound can go on for a long time beyond one's exhalation of breath.

In the top photograph my dead grandmother moves a fraction of an inch. She lifts the tip of her smallest finger.

Friday

I decide today my dead relatives will be in their thirties, meaning today they will be younger than me, meaning they are younger than me yet dead, and alive, and beautiful in the way that people in old photographs are beautiful, their skin a smooth warm sepia, their dresses made of shadows and light.

Specifically, my dead grandma Stella is dressed for a day at the carnival, a cluster of imitation pearls around her neck.

My dead grandma Helen wears a dusky nail polish and a striped sheath dress, a wreath of flowers in her hair.

My dead aunt carries a white handbag.

They look familiar, like people I know or knew.

They look so young.

They are so young and bored.

In front of us the lake's stubby waves form then unform.

My dead relatives pick the dirt out from beneath their thickened fingernails and flick the dirt across the ground.

The sun must be going down though it is more a sense of darkening happening in the west, to our right.

'Are you ready for your surgery?' my dead aunt Mary asks.

'No,' I tell her.

She combs her fingers through her hair, which is wild and windswept. I think it's still her real hair.

The picnic pavilion looks the same as it did the previous day.

I am tired of describing the pavilion.

The trees shudder. This is the last Friday I'll have breasts.

Earlier today I was thinking of time machines.

I was thinking, if I had a time machine, I would use it this very minute to go back through time and tell my dead grandmothers and my dead aunt, at the age they are now, between thirty-five and forty years old, to remove their ovaries, and fallopian tubes, and uterus, and cervix, and I would recommend they remove their breasts as well, before these body parts could kill them. Then I would warn their cousins and their siblings. Then I would go back further in time and warn my great-grandmother then I'd warn my great-grandmother's brothers and sisters, as well as their potentially pathogenic decedents. Then whoever came before my great-grandmother, I would warn them too. I don't know who they are but, if I had a time machine, I would find out who they are and I would warn them. 'Beware of ovaries!' I would say. 'Beware of breasts, both male and female, and fallopian tubes, and the peritoneum, and prostates, and possibly the pancreas!'

'Time machines aren't real,' points out my dead grandma Helen.

'I know. It's just a fantasy I have, saving all those people.'

'Do you want to sit on my lap, dear?' asks my dead grandma Stella. She pets the tops of her thighs, the place where I would sit were I a child.

In the only photo I remember of her and me, I am one year old, on her lap, the cancer already spread; she is wearing a wig. She died before my second birthday.

She must have such few memories of me.

'I'm not a baby anymore, Grandma,' I remind her.

She laughs, shakes her head, fingers her necklace. 'My mistake!'

Looking at her is like looking at a different version of myself, only this version is dead.

'Are we helping you feel better, dear?'

No, they are not helping me feel better today.

My dead grandma suggests we watch a video of a double mastectomy. Perhaps that might calm my nerves?

We watch the video together on my phone.

The video claims to be 1 minute 45 seconds in length though it feels longer.

I find the visuals difficult to describe though, at the same time, I feel compelled to describe them.

The interior of a woman's breast is: brain-like? gelatinous? yellow? red? bulbous? bloody? squishy? jiggly? deadly? alien? spongy? pliable? shiny? soft? otherworldly? inhuman? human? sexual? asexual? moldable? shapeless? well-lit? intimate? luminescent? lustrous? cancerous? pre-cancerous? close to the heart? dabbed off? eyeless?

'Shhh. It's okay,' whispers my dead aunt Mary, switching off my phone.

I can tell she's lying by the way she plays with her hair.

I keep losing their shapes, the outlines of their bodies, in the near dark.

I would have liked to know my grandmothers.

I would have liked to have more family stories.

My dead relatives ask me, since these are the last days I will be relatively complete, do I want to destroy something.

I say yes, I would like to destroy something.

The top of the picnic pavilion detonates into splintered wood.

The playground is lifted into the air and thrown away.

The paths along the lake fracture apart swallowing all the ovaries and uteruses and breasts of the exercising, and it is bloody.

After the monster rises out of the lake, there are pieces of people, women, trees, lakes, organs, everywhere.

'Good job, dear,' say my dead relatives.

At home, I open my dead grandmother's copy of *Your Dreams and Your Horoscope: 25,000 Interpretations of the Messages Received in Sleep and the Predictions of the Stars, Planets and other Heavenly Bodies*. It is the only book I have of hers.

Under GHOST: 'Signifies the immediate need of powerful resistance against the ill will of a group of people who are plotting your ruin.'

Under CANCER: 'Although it might seem to point otherwise, a dream of this disease portends an improvement in health.'

Under SURGEON: 'The augury is of an improvement in health.'

Under GRANDMOTHER: 'An omen of plenty.'

Under ILLNESS: 'Arguments with those you love are predicted by any dream of being ill; if it is others who are ill, the augury is of distress through worry.'

Under GUILT: nothing listed.

Under REGRET: nothing.

Under ANGER: 'Either good or bad – good if the anger is roused by injustice; bad if merely an exhibition of temper.'

Under STERILITY: nothing.

Under SUNSET: 'Gorgeous colors in the sky at sunset are a prophecy of a new opportunity to make good with your wife, husband, sweetheart, or employer.'

Under DEAD FOLK: 'To dream of conversing with dead people is a propitious omen, signifying strength, courage, and a clear conscience.'

Under BREAST: 'See BOSOM.'

Under BOSOM: 'If a young woman dreams that her bosom is hurt, some calamity will overtake her. If she dreams of a flat or wrinkled bosom, she may expect to be heartbroken.'

Saturday

'I donated my bathing suit today and all my bras,' I tell my dead grandmothers and my dead aunt beside the ruins of the picnic pavilion by the lake.

The county park staff have swept up the worst of the viscera. This morning they stretched a blue tarp across the damaged pavilion roof. The tarp flaps in the wind, providing a weak yet protective structure. My dead relatives are wearing comfortable dresses, elastic and dark knit, and easy to clean, their bright slips showing below the hems, the kind of outfit one wears outside to run along a sidewalk after two young children.

'It was surprisingly emotional to put my bras into a box. I mean, I cried,' I tell them.

My dead relatives glance at each other, worried.

'There will be harder parts than this, dear,' says my dead aunt Mary.

'This is not the hardest part,' she adds

She is out of focus today. They all are, their edges permeable to the wind, the leaves.

I list off the supplies I've gathered in a pile in my bedroom to use during the weeks of recovery after my breasts are severed from me.

I have the feeling that I am leaving my gender behind me in a trail of patented robes and surgical drain belts and memory-foam wedge pillows.

'My, look how organized you are!' one of my dead grandmothers says. I make her say this.

At times I don't care about what I'm leaving behind me, more curious about what I will become.

Sometimes I care.

I imagine my husband cares.

How did their own husbands feel, I ask my dead relatives, about intimacy, after –

'Remember the scars were bigger with us. From the navel on down . . .'

'Above the navel to the pubic hair. It was not entirely pleasant.'

'I would recommend, when the time comes, keeping on your shirt,' says one of them.

I am trying not to look behind me.

My surgery begins in thirty-six hours.

My dead aunt and my dead grandmothers gossip about what to wear to the operating theater Monday morning, either their pale vintage hospital gowns with the geometric flower patterns or the two-piece blazer and skirt sets they would have worn to Sunday Mass.

The sun is already setting. It feels like here the sun is always setting, as if setting once can never be enough. Over and over and over the sun is setting, casting its perpetual shadows.

The film skips; the images jump, settle, blur.

I sigh and open my orange notebook, where I had written down questions one is supposed to ask of dead relatives in the days before major surgery.

'Oh look at her with her little notebook and pen,' says one of my dead grandmothers.

I read the questions aloud.

The questions relate to their childhoods and whether or not they went to the Chicago World's Fair.

My dead grandma Helen lights a cigarette even though I've told her smoking is no longer considered healthy or sophisticated.

'Children should be seen and not heard,' she says, exhaling.

Smoke leaks from the hole in her chest; it looks like she is smoldering.

The questions are stupid. I throw my notebook into the lake.

Notebooks, mine anyway, don't float.

'I wish I could actually talk to you,' I say.

'You are talking to us.'

'I know so little of your lives. The stories I know are, like, you might have graduated from high school, Grandma Stella. My mom said she can't imagine why you wouldn't have.'

'And then what happened?'

'That's the whole story.'

My phone buzzes with a new text from my mom.

'Excuse me. My mom just got back to me. It looks like maybe you didn't graduate from high school. We don't know for sure. If you didn't go to high school, what did you do? Did you meet my grandfather young? Did you get a job? If you didn't get a job, what did you do?'

'I'm not going to tell you. I guess you will never know!' says my dead grandma Stella in a sing-song voice as if I am a child and this is a fun game and we are playing the game.

The deterioration of film: when the chemical bonding begins to break down, the solid becomes a gas, the gas leaves a void –

'What should we do now? Should we bake a cake? Should we sing a song? Should we dance the foxtrot?' asks my dead grandma Helen, inhaling, exhaling.

I request an hour alone with my dead grandmother Stella, who I have wondered about in particular throughout my life. Out of this trio of dead women I knew her least, meaning not at all. Yet we share a last name. We share the pathogenic variant. These have to be intimacies.

These have to be golden threads connecting her throat to my throat, her abdomen to my abdomen.

'What a bunch of baloney,' says my dead grandma Helen. Insulted, she swallows her cigarette and she and my dead aunt stomp off to the shore of the lake where they pick up rocks. They throw the rocks at the cormorants, who rise up in a disarray of black wings. When the birds are gone, they drop additional rocks into the pockets of their dresses and wade into the water. I would be worried about them only they're already dead and anyway I can't save them.

My dead grandma Stella is staring at me.

She is staring at my face, my neck, my arms, my hands, my ankles, my waist, my breasts.

After she married, she lived for years with her growing family on South Wallace Street in Chicago in a brick home constructed in 1915 with a rounded front door.

I know this and other minor details – the rounded front door has a six-panel window in it – because I have been researching what I can find of her in the evenings.

There are so few mentions in online databases of anyone with her maiden name. I think I found her father in a tax listing in Galesburg, Illinois. That's all. Though in Springfield, Illinois, there was a man with her married name who, in 1946, shot another man over a bill, shot him in the stomach and in the leg, and the injured man died, so the man with her married name was charged with murder. That man has nothing to do with my dead grandmother as far as I could tell. I found the census records that mention her. She is mentioned on line 31 in 1920 and line 28 in 1930 and line 33 in 1940 for a total of three lines. I found her death certificate. She died at 10.44 p.m. on 24 April. On the night she died, the moon was waxing crescent, the dew point was 23.33, the visibility was fifteen miles, the sun had risen at 5.57 a.m. and set at 7.42 p.m., and the max wind speed was thirteen miles per hour. Photographs of the hospital where she died show a dignified brick building designed by Eben Ezra Roberts in the Beaux Arts/neoclassical style and built in 1911–12 with multiple brick chimneys, though there were later additions. My grandmother probably entered the hospital through the historic 1927 limestone entrance on North Austin Boulevard that has since been enclosed. A contemporary of Frank Lloyd Wright, architect E.E. Roberts grew up in Massachusetts with a woodcarver for a father. In addition to this hospital, he designed an ice-skating rink, a high school, almost 200 residential homes and a local amusement park whose rides included Chase Through the Clouds and Leap the Dips –

My dead grandmother pats my shoulder.

'I can tell you worked very hard on that project. Good job,' she says.

'I named my daughter after you,' I tell her. 'She has a porcelain plate you decorated.'

'The plate with the wild roses,' remembers my dead grandmother. She smells of allspice and decay. I don't want this to be an essay about me imagining her.

'You are not making this up,' my dead grandmother assures me.

This is the last Saturday I will have breasts.

'I want you to keep haunting me after my surgery,' I say.

Embarrassed, she looks away from me toward the lake.

Her image jitters as if the sprocket holes have been damaged on the film reel due to careless handling.

She is not that type of ghost.

I would raise her from the dead myself if I could.

'Well, you kind of are, dear,' she says.

The remnants of other people's fires shift inside the pedestal grills in the breeze.

We put our heads together.

The sun sets.

I realize she isn't breathing.

'Oh honey, I don't have to,' she whispers.

In one of the pictures I am sitting at the piano wearing my dead grandmother's wedding dress. I am ten years old, sitting on the piano bench, my dead grandmother's veil in my hair.

Sunday

The American robins rebuild their nests in the pavilion ruins.

The ground surrounding the pavilion is pockmarked and uneven.

The exercising women have not yet returned to the path along the lake and maybe they never will, scared now of the water or what lies beneath the water, as they should be.

'Are you ready for your big day tomorrow?' asks my dead aunt Mary with enthusiasm.

My dead relatives are wearing their practical house dresses again, inexpensive and easy to launder, what women wear when they're among family. Their details have grown softened around the edges and blurred, which I have said before.

'No, I'm not ready,' I say.

The sun is setting but it hasn't yet set.

It seems to be taking longer than usual to set today.

I don't think I will ever be ready.

When you are not ready to lose something, yet you lose it anyway, this creates a *rip in one's heart*.

I am not speaking metaphorically. The heart actually rips.

My dead grandma Helen, it turns out, is not my only relative with a hole in her chest.

There is the smell of vinegar.

When, after my surgery tomorrow, I will close my eyes to rest, I will see a scalpel slicing across the mound of my breasts or what was once my breasts, and wide, open flaps of skin.

In the recovery room, when I wake, my dead grandmothers will hurry to hide the spray of my blood on their gowns.

'Hush, don't even think about that now.'

My dead aunt reaches to stroke my hair, the motion more like a sound than a touch. It's like I'm talking to a row of shadows.

The sky is fearful and angry and sad.

'Six months from now, really, you will hardly remember all this.'

'You'll hardly remember us, I imagine.'

'Yes, what has it been, twenty years since you last talked to me in a story?'

'She has never talked to me in a story.'

'Me neither.'

The wind turns red. The red wind blows their red house dresses around but gently, less critically than before. Their pain hangs around their shoulders today, wrapping around their necks like proud necklaces of fog.

'I'm sorry,' I say, which is all along what I had wanted to say to them because when this essay ends, and I know it will soon end, I will be alive, and they will not be alive, and I will be unable to pretend otherwise.

'Oh my, enough long faces,' proclaims my dead aunt Mary. 'Let's dissect some owl pellets and see what we can find among the bones!'

Using forceps and probes, we identify the small quills of a bird and the protective wing casing of a beetle.

In another picture, my older sister and my grandmother Helen are seated on a metal bench out on the patio. My grandmother is asleep in the backyard while my older sister shows off her Birthstones and Blossoms doll. It is thirty-four years ago. It is my older sister's twelfth birthday. This is my sister who also has the pathogenic variant and who will, also, go on to lose her ovaries and her fallopian tubes and her uterus. This is the year my grandmother is going to die. She's already, mostly, dead, the tumor long ago having burst through the walls of her ovaries into other interiors. But she isn't dead yet. The night before my surgery, my grandmother in the picture wakes up. I wake her up. My residual anger and fear wake her up. She opens her eyes. She screams. She has done this before, the screaming, only this time the sound is generative, like a creation song. It is the kind of song only a dead woman with a tumor can make for her granddaughter with a pathogenic variant the night before the granddaughter's double mastectomy. The song is powerful, calling forth clouds and a new moon and more owls and planets and lightning and flooding and daughters. By singing this song she is teaching me how to sing this song, in case I must sing it myself one day to my own daughter or my own granddaughter. A song that destroys bodies then rebuilds them. Part lullaby, part dirge, part family story. ∎

The first meal was breakfast, as it must have been morning by then. I ate the doughy pancake with one hand, using my plastic fork to shovel in the spongy eggs with the other. I heard the woman on the other side of the curtain complain that she didn't get a meal. She had an Eastern European accent. The nurse checked her clipboard. She was not on the list for solid meals. Why, she had not had anesthesia. I felt solidarity with her irritation. We must have delivered around the same time. There was that scream down the hall, awful in its velocity. It sounded like someone being murdered. I wonder what I sounded like, whether my voice was recognizable as the animal I had been. Sometime in the night my roommate had asked a nurse in low tones to have the baby taken to the nursery. The babies kept on squawking. I drifted in and out, listening for cries. Mine slept most of the time, and I let her. There was no one there, like last time, to wake me up every hour to nurse. They were understaffed or keeping away. I spoke to the baby out loud, as I leaned over the transparent bassinet, ineptly wrapping her in the soft hospital blanket, creamy with pink and blue stripes, not as expert as the nurse's swaddle. A reassuring patter, to keep myself awake, so as not to drop her. I wasn't terrified this time around to be alone with the baby. I liked looking at her, the funny striped hat covering dark tufts of hair, her red chubby cheeks mottled with white, like wax, her eyes closed, the purse of her mouth which I positioned against my deep brown aureole, my breast the size of her face, her tummy with the yellowing umbilical cord like latex clamped with plastic, pressed against my hard swollen belly. I stroked her skinny bird legs. My husband must have left by then to go pick up our child from the house where she was staying, friends willing to risk possible contagion. Perhaps I was speaking to the baby out loud to remind myself that I was a person. The effect was getting to me, not seeing any other faces. When footsteps approached I learned to quickly push up my mask. I heard my roommate being admonished for not having hers on correctly. I pieced together from a phone conversation that she also had a child around the same age as my firstborn. Later her husband smuggled her food in a bag, from outside, it smelled unimaginably delicious. Hamburger and fries. Someone else must have been watching their other child while her husband visited. Her mother perhaps. Maybe a nanny. They murmured companionably, and I saw their feet in the makeshift room surrounded by curtains on wires. I shuffled my body across the floor to perform my ablutions, hoping the baby wouldn't wake – the peppermint oil in the basin, the inching down the mesh panties, squeezing the peri bottle into the urine stream to lessen burning, cleaning blood off the floor, off the plastic bottle, all the waste into the garbage, washing the blood from my hands. Trying to get myself back in the bed, to get my swollen feet out of my white foam shoes, swing my leaden legs up and arrange the sheets. I was freezing, I kept on asking for a blanket – the nurse would come by and admonish me that the baby wasn't more covered up, she was just wearing a diaper, I couldn't figure out the snaps on the baby's kimono. More meals came, signaled by a sun I could not see, the blinds down, and the overhead lights coldly fluorescent. A slice of turkey breast and mashed potatoes, strange for the end of summer, how white it was on the styrofoam plate. After the woman's husband visited I heard a new voice on the other side of the curtain, a nurse who didn't come see me. I wondered if they had hired an attendant. She showered my roommate with compliments, and I was able to piece together more about her. You are so beautiful, she would say to her. You are so tall and slim, you must be a model. How is it possible, that you have just given birth? I gleaned that her husband played basketball professionally. I had gotten a sense that they were tall. I noticed their large feet under the curtain as I hurried by, glancing briefly through the opening. I think she was sitting up in a chair, wearing a lounge set. There was something swannish about them. The mirror at the sink, my face jaundiced and puffy, my lips chapped. Throughout the day we toggled through the various protocols that would allow us to leave. The hearing test. The pediatrician's visit. The hospital representative who asked me a series of questions about my care I answered in the affirmative. First they'd visit the woman, then I'd wait for them to come to me. The lactation consultant, with kind, mascaraed eyes, came to me first. I appreciated that she touched the baby's head tenderly when situating us on the pillows, watching me latch. It felt painful still, but I didn't say anything. We spoke about her daughter's preschool. I was just grateful to make small talk. I heard my roommate worry that the baby wasn't latching right. She was sure, she said that her baby had a tongue-tie, her first one had it as well. The consultant listened and spoke with her, and I listened too. Once the woman on the other side heard me petitioning to leave the next morning, asking what else needed to be done of the requisite testing and paperwork, she began requesting the same. Once we were approved to leave, I began packing up my things, moving slowly around the bed. At one point I heard her voice through the curtain. I wanted to wish you luck with everything, she said. I wished the same to her. I imagine I would never recognize her, if I saw her out in the world, with her two children, our youngest the same age, as I never saw her face. ■

Dawn Watson

The Starlings of Dunmore Died on the Eleventh of July

July 1988

1

I heard them hit the ground like pound coins falling
out of trouser pockets. They must have followed me
home from Alexandra Park.

2

The noise woke me. I tottered to the window on stilts,
scanning the street for the source of the dings and stints.
It was too hot and too light for ten o'clock, even in July.
I pressed my forehead to the glass. My skin made a halo.
Outside, the dented street light was orange and fizzing.
The entry's white-painted posts were dark blue. Ruptured
footpath slabs cast more than five shadows off kerbs
and cracks along Skegoneill Drive. Black was thrown
in all directions. I couldn't see to the bottom of the street,
even with my cheek to the pane. I knew it was the birds.

3

I had spent the day in the park. I'd looked at the food
in Crazy Prices on the Antrim Road until I got cold,
then cut down Jubilee Avenue to the vast entrance.
The four stone gate pillars are giant. Small, startled
flowers are carved into the rock. The whole shebang
is a fearful wasteland of bricks, rust, prongs and spikes,
lined with heavy sycamores. Alexandra Park carries
the smell of old graveyard badness about it. It tips up a hill
and falls away to the Protestant end. An interface descent
over the strict white bridge into trees as stepped and steep
as the unsteady, brick-full stream slicing through it.

4

A couple of long summers back, wee Jim Benson fell off
the park's metal hexagon climbing frame onto concrete.
His leg broke under him with a sound like a crisp packet
getting stood on. His aunt ran over, sprung from the row
of big Victorian houses set like overbearing maths jotters
opposite the stone gate posts. Her mouth, fixed in a square,
emitted a weary yow-ow-ow. In a panic, our mate Sam
had tried to climb the hard, green railings growing tall
out of thick border walls that forever pushed the park
below footpath level in its sunken north-east corner.
The railings had curved spikes like horns.

5

Today, I had summoned the birds without thinking.
Clock seeds blew over patches of melted tarmac, gravel
and tin cans where fires were set and settled in the park.
Not enough air, despite the cold sweeping down over
the houses from the Cavehill, where they crucified Jesus.
Green space left to be green when it shouldn't have been.
Trails from an inner perimeter weaved down to the path.
Invisible ways in and out, gaps. Handsome pan-loaf bags
tied to the desperate railings round the lake. Paint peeling.
The flock of starlings was hovering over the water.

6

I hid on the secret lane and spoke over the marsh reeds,
over the concrete dock, to the cloud of blattering wings.
I said to them, *What are youse doin', what are youse doin',
what are youse doin'?*

7

Later, I sallied over the bridge to my granny's house
on the Limestone Road. On to my aunt Marjorie's house
in Mountcollyer. You say it *Marjee's*. Every Eleventh,
she lit a kids boney in the burnt-out Castleton playground
on the York Road. Melted benches were more violent
than the cheerful swings on fire on bright metal strings.

8

On the way home, I cut past the park, up the worn, bent
concrete steps to Gainsborough Drive. The iron banister
had delicate, welded metal balls to stop you sliding down.
You can see the docks from the top; Samson and Goliath,
the gantry cranes, the old brown mill off the Shore Road,
all unfolded and creased into life like a pop-up Bible.

9

Before I went to bed, Tom Loudon was in the living room
telling my mum to do the double. He was a drunk man
with a long dog called Tiny. I decided to poison him
when I was told to make him tea. He was shouting
and so was my mum. He had a mole on his face
the colour of dirt. It moved up when he grinned,
like he was holding his teeth up for you to see.
I poured Brasso in the bottom of the cup.
He didn't notice and neither did she.

10

Now, the house was empty. I listened for rumble voices.
The *dada-dun-dun-dun* of 'Another One Bites the Dust'
had stopped rifling through the floor. The party was over.
I pressed my big toe into my bedroom's red carpet pile
and it nearly sucked me under. On the walls, cut and stuck
pages from *Metal Hammer*, *Hit Parade* and *Kerrang!*
fill every space. Steve Harris was the ugly face of metal.
I left my room lit by street light, slipped onto the landing.

11

The stairs smelled of cigarettes. The toilet was gurgling.
The adults had spilled to the dogs. From down the street,
the tin crack of the dog trap in Dunmore Stadium came
spiralling through the open front door. I heard a faint cheer
and pictured the giddy crowds in the wooden stands alight.
It was a week after Toy Boy won the high-flown record
for the fastest dog of 1988. The race ground was sand.
It was like they were at the beach. The whole shebang
tumbled behind a tall green metal fence. From the street,
you could just about see the top of a gigantic floodlight.
Its beautiful white blaze didn't even try to spill over.

12

Yesterday, I had woken in the night with a bang.
I jumped up, ran to the top of the stairs, and sat down.
I gripped the banister at the blackened thumbprint.
Someone had touched the white gloss before it was dry.
The whorls and swirls gathered dirt. A clatter sprang
clean from downstairs. Do you want me to hit you?
said my dad. The yellowed skirting board was scuffed.
The paint was chipped off in the shape of Australia.
I moved halfway down the stairs. The living room
door was wide open. My dad stood over my mum
with the poker. She was crouched between the settee
and the magazine rack. Her arms were fixed above
her head. She dropped them to whisper at my dad.
Her blonde hair was over to one side. The poker hit
the wall. She squeezed her head towards her chest.
I sailed downstairs and jumped off the third last stair.
I ran in and drew my shoulders up to my ears.

13

Daddy, don't! He looked like the moon
looks in the daytime. My mum dropped her arms.
In a normal voice, like she would speak to the postman,
she said, John stop, John. Maxine's up out of bed.
She waved like I was leaving. He dropped the poker.
He grabbed her hair and pulled her into the hall
Her foot hit an empty Bacardi bottle and it rolled
under the settee. I said, Stop. My dad tried to drag
my mum upstairs. His curly hair was radioactive.
He shouted, You did, Jean. You know you did.
She kicked out at him. He fell back, then stood up
and walked to the kitchen. The back door slammed.
My mum touched her head as if it was impossible
she was real. Get out of the house, love, she said.
Run to the corner. There was blood on her brow
in the shape of a tired giraffe. I ran down the steps
and up the street.

14

Tonight, the street was orange and smelled of smoke.
Telephone wires fritzed overhead, big news of damage
from street pyres, from peeler to Brit, and mum to dad,
and granny to aunt to neighbour. Did you see the one
down the York Road, sure, someone would always say.
The swings would be melted. There were the remains
of a digger on fire on the corner of Ashfield Gardens
from a street party earlier. The bonfire was still lit
on top of a sheet of corrugated metal in the middle
of Glandore Parade. Nothing could get down it now.
It was a short street. I walked beneath the last sparks
of the bonfire. The rippled and patched concrete road
was a bean-feast of beer cans, beach chairs and ripped
burger buns. Sadie's gate creaked in number seven.
Blind Scruff barked. A late-season wasp circled
the shrunken black privets. The big light went out
in number three. Wee Jim's blue BMX was tangled
in plastic bunting. I used to borrow it when he let me.
Then his dad said, Get your own bike.

15

Skegoneill Drive dead-ends with the fence separating us
from Dunmore Stadium. Underneath was a long dry bed
of dirt about one-foot high held up by a short brick wall.
On the ground were two hundred dead starlings dropped
out of the sky.

16

The birds were on car bonnets, on kerbs and on hedges.
There was a bird on a cheese and onion crisp packet.
There were about ten birds on Mrs Heron's garden path.
There was one on a blue Cortina with one eye shut,
beak slack like it was looking through a telescope.

17

The birds were on the road. They were lying in patches
and curves and ones and twos and fours. Face down,
side down, all along the gutter. The dying bonfire
behind me was indifferent. All around, the starlings
were puffed-up and pinched as though holding
their breath and wondering why help doesn't come
to small things.

18

I dug dirt graves under the fence with a lolly stick.
The traps went smack, slap-smack. Who cares?
I tell the birds, It's not your fault, it's theirs.
Their feet bones stuck up like RTE aerials,
wings crossed, eyes rolled back and open.

MANU FERNEINI
Inside the newsroom of *An-Nahar*, Lebanon's national newspaper, three kilometres away from the site of the explosion at the Port of Beirut, 8 August 2020

BEIRUT FRAGMENTS, 2021

Charif Majdalani

TRANSLATED FROM THE FRENCH
BY RUTH DIVER

1

All at once, it comes back to me: a light touch, fluid, fleeting, hanging discreetly somewhere in the air. Suddenly it starts to play, as if drawn out of hiding; it waves at me then disappears when I pay attention, then comes back and finally settles in, as if to show me that it wasn't just a mirage. That's when I understand that this is it, that I'm recovering my sense of smell, and that right now, in fact, I am smelling the scent of jasmine. I feel so happy, so grateful, that I hardly dare breathe, as if I might be punished, this perfume confiscated again. But no, it really is here, subtle and delicate, and with it the whole world is restored to me. Again I realise what the loss of smell and taste involves, how it deprives reality of its fullness, its depth, its consistency. It's as if an entire dimension had been kept in shadow, within arm's reach but always escaping me, unattainable, frustrating. And then comes the day I decide to take some cortisone, just a little, a few grams, because this has nothing to do with Covid, it's just my chronic rhinitis depriving me of smell and taste. Two days after the first dose that palette of fine sensations, those subtle marvels, make their first appearance, like the scent of jasmine as I opened the garden gate, which seemed to call out to me then go into hiding, to return and settle simultaneously within and without me, reconnecting me to the world.

Today I tasted peppermint chocolate, I tasted a fresh ripe peach. I smelled the jasmine in the garden and the gardenia on the terrace. And also the violent industrial diesel from the tanker that was pumping water to the roof of the building next door, and the ghastly sour stench of refuse that sometimes floats over the city, depending on the direction of the wind.

2

I can't help thinking that this stench is the smell of the corpse we are living with, the corpse of the state, of this dead country, or at least of the one we used to know.

3

In the year since the port blast, the oligarchs in power still haven't formed a government. It's been two years since the economic crisis began, and not a single reform, not a single measure, not a single decision has been taken. Abandoned, the country is floundering, and what the most twisted, pessimistic minds predicted is now taking place: there is no electricity at all any more. The power rationed out by the state network has been cut off, and everything now depends on neighbourhood generators. These need fuel, but diesel has disappeared, leading to the rationing of private electricity production. Whole neighbourhoods are gradually going dark. The hospitals have no fuel either, there are shortages of drugs and the pharmacies are empty. And there is no petrol, of course. Beirut's legendary traffic jams have disappeared, except around the petrol stations that are still selling, where incredible queues of cars block streets and avenues. We live with the permanent sense of imminent disaster.

4

Our internet connection is getting worse. Sometimes there is hardly any at all for hours at a time.

Ogero, the company that manages the telecommunications network, announced that it could no longer guarantee the operation of the Akkar and Chouf exchanges because of the shortage of fuel.

I called the water-truck company for a delivery, because our tanks are empty. The guy who answered, a Syrian man, told me that he could come, of course, that he was at my service, but that he no longer had diesel for the pump that sends the water to the tanks on the roof.

5

Artists, stylists, designers, film-makers, doctors, psychologists, radiologists are leaving in their hundreds. People who have no qualifications are trying to leave too.

To get a new passport you have to wait up to fifteen hours in the government departments, which are barely operating for lack of electricity, or simply because there is no paper for the forms and official documents. Civil servants are no longer turning up to work; they don't have the petrol to drive, or they've decided their salaries aren't worth coming in for any more.

The ministry of the interior issues a warning about the increasing number of desertions from the police.

6

This morning, as I was sitting on the terrace trying to write the answers to some interview questions while at the same time discreetly observing my son, I wondered what kind of future he might have in this country that the journalist was asking me about, and even if there was any future at all here for him or his sister. With the economic collapse, the political destruction of Lebanon, the ecological and structural scarring of the country, and the rising power of obscure, malevolent, retrograde political forces, I ask myself every day what kind of country, what kind of legacy, we are leaving our children.

7

The generator in the Anid family's building has broken down from overuse. In the neighbourhood where my friends the Naïms live, the supplier has stopped providing power because of the lack of fuel. My colleague Roula posts on Facebook that there is only forty-five minutes' worth of electricity per day at her place. Her supplier's generator overheated, then stopped working. Another operator had been promising a connecting line for the last three weeks, and then told her that his generator wouldn't cope with any more demand. A third replied that she lived too far away, that she mustn't be angry with him, he has too many calls on his generator as well, and anyway, he'll soon have to stop supplying electricity and turn his generators off, they can't run day and night, and soon there will be no more fuel.

Up until this morning, I thought we'd been lucky with our electricity supply. Our neighbourhood, between Furn el Chebbak and Badaro, has two suppliers. One of them rations power, and seems on the verge of cutting off all supply. But the other sells power to our building, and seemed to be still holding out. This morning though, at dawn, the purring of the air conditioner suddenly stopped. The silence that replaced it took on a sinister significance. I stayed in bed for a long time with my eyes open, immobile. I could sense that my wife understood the silence too. I flicked the light switch next to the bed, but nothing happened.

For the first time, we are no longer able to turn on the stove, to charge our phones, or to use our landline. The fridges no longer work, and the heat is stifling. But all that, strangely, is less distressing than one thing we had not expected, or even thought about, until we were faced with it: the impossibility of raising the electric blinds on the windows. That's what I found most intensely depressing, like a symbol of the dark pit in which we are now all trapped.

8

The economic crisis that brought an end to the thirty years of the Second Republic in Lebanon – which was itself born after the fifteen-year-long civil war – was the result of the political caste's overwhelming stranglehold on the state and its mechanisms, and of their monumental corruption. But this huge criminal operation, along with the no-less-gigantic fraud that our banking system has turned out to be, was in fact nothing more than the inescapable consequence of the civil war. Those in power thirty years after the end of the conflict were the militia leaders themselves, who had simply mutated into politicians. They brought their client base and former members of staff to power, and continued with the course of action they'd developed during the war – mafia practices and communitarian factionalism – with the sole aim of enriching themselves and acquiring more power, first with the support of the occupying Syrian forces, then alone, under Hezbollah's protection. They had no plans, no ambition to reconstruct the country in any real sense, or to learn any lessons from the failings of the First Republic.

The men who contributed to destroying the country during the war succeeded only after thirty years of peace.

9

It's been a year now since foreign currency deposits have been inaccessible. For months the banks have been restricting withdrawals in local currency too. Everyone is convinced that we will never see our money again. Those who still hold accounts, notably in dollars, only have one way to recoup a small portion of their assets, a route that is also used by retailers in order to trade. The process is bizarre. It consists in writing cheques and selling them for cash at 10 or 15 per cent of their value – in other words, at a massive loss. I was not the only one wondering who might be profiting from these kinds of transactions, and how. In the end it was a lawyer we met one evening at the Menassas' who explained how it all works. The dealers buy the cheques at ten times less than their value, then resell them for cash, with a small margin, to the banks themselves, who then wipe the entire sum from their books. It's an insidious stratagem called a 'haircut', which allows the banks to liquidate their clients' accounts.

One week ago I tried to sell a cheque myself. The currency dealer I use often takes care of these sorts of transactions. Like many of his colleagues he no longer opens his shop, but visits clients at home instead. My dealer is a young man, sturdy, talkative, with a slightly louche swagger, and he hops around when he is negotiating or counting his bundles of banknotes. It's difficult to get him to sit down. He's a sly devil, keeps trying to convince me that he is making terrible sacrifices and losing money by giving me preferential rates, which I know is not the case. One day, a few months ago, I noticed that he was limping. He told me he fell off his moped. I asked him whether it was wise to ride around on a moped with panniers full of dollars and Lebanese pounds. He replied that it was safer than a car because in a car you might get stuck in a traffic jam, or blocked in by another car, while on a moped you're always able to escape an ambush attempt. As for his limp, he had smashed into a car door that a young woman had carelessly opened in front of him while he was speeding like a madman. He flew over the door and landed on the other side, and while people were trying to help him up, asking him how he was, the young woman suggesting she call an ambulance, all he could think about was that he needed to stay calm, to behave as if nothing had happened, so that he could go back to the carcass of his moped with its pannier stuffed full of banknotes.

So, a week ago I tried to sell a cheque. I wanted to empty our accounts once and for all, and to start work on the land we had bought in the mountains, and into which we had poured our funds from the bank. Over the phone, my dealer offered to buy the cheque for 13 per cent of its value. The next day cheques in dollars were worth 13.5 per cent. My dealer laughed, as if he found this lottery funny, then reminded me that the rate for cheques was pegged to the dollar on the black market. And that he thought it might go even higher. But that evening, the cheque was only worth 12 per cent. The next day 11.5 per cent. By the time the fellow turned up at my place and paid me my miserable amount, I had lost another half percentage point. The dealer, as if to cheer me up, announced jovially that he was getting engaged. His offhandedness annoyed me so much that I didn't even try to pretend to be interested. But then he surprised me: his fiancée was the young woman whose car door had almost sent him to his death.

10

The most pressing question remains: why do people accept what is happening to them? Why did the uprising have no effect, and why did it come to such a sudden end? The answer is simple. When the street protests stopped it was because of a lack of vision, of alternative plans, or even common cause. This itself is the result of the actions the ruling caste have taken over the last thirty years. They systematically undermined the trade unions, infiltrating and controlling professional associations until all had been reduced to silence. Of course those are the very organisations that might have been able to mobilise demonstrations. Their destruction has left only the communitarian political parties – the oligarchy's base – as an operational organising force. If the new organisations and groups set up after the 2019 uprising fail to find a way forward, most of those who participated in the protests will gradually return to the traditional parties.

11

The 2019 uprising and the months that followed did at least lay a foundation for the Lebanese people to have a sense of citizenship. The history of democracies – from antiquity and the Athenian experiment to modern times – has shown that citizenship is built from the wreckage of the affiliation to clan, tribe and communitarian groups, replacing older allegiances which, in time, are supposed to weaken and disappear. In Lebanon, no matter how hard we try to build a sense of common citizenship, those old allegiances resurface at the slightest instability, almost as a reflex. Citizens seek refuge in older ties of loyalty, becoming once again members of their own communities and facing off against other communities, instead of remaining side by side as citizens of a democratic state. We now fear new instability, perhaps provoked by the political parties themselves (in the form of communitarian strife) in order to bring their followers back into the fold, positioning themselves as the foundation and rampart of their own groups. Those who took part in the 2019 uprising, that moment which seemed to forge a new sense of citizenship, will eventually return to their clans and communities and traditional political leaders.

They will forget the corruption, the bankruptcy, the collapse and the port blast. And all will be lost.

12

For a month now I've been trying to avoid going to the pharmacy, even for the simplest medicines. The first time my pharmacist announced that she didn't have any more of the medication I take for my chronic rhinitis, I felt a sense of dread, of abandonment, of being caught in a trap. It was a bit like the first time I realised that I could no longer withdraw money from the bank, that my deposits had probably disappeared forever. But yesterday afternoon my son started to get a sore throat. We were anxious at the thought that he might have strep throat, because we remembered that we hadn't taken the precaution of buying antibiotics in advance.

We went to ten different pharmacies to try to find antibiotics. Some pharmacists didn't dare look us in the eye, others were like beaten dogs. One of them, however, hesitated briefly. I sensed that he might have one or two boxes in reserve for urgent cases. He asked whether my son had a fever, and when I answered that he didn't *yet* have a temperature, he suddenly pretended to double-check his computer, and I could tell that I'd missed out. And indeed, he confirmed that he didn't have any antibiotics.

All this is nothing compared to the diabetic patients with no dialysis, and the cancer patients with no treatment, to say nothing of the insurance companies that are not paying out any more, or the social security system that has definitively failed, or the fact that there is no more cash anyway and bank accounts are now worthless.

13

The lack of petrol creates absurd situations. On some thoroughfares the traffic still moves, and yesterday afternoon, while bringing my son back from a friend's place, we drove home through Mazraa. I have never seen that avenue so empty. Nadim said that it reminded him of lockdown. And then suddenly, in other places, monstrous traffic jams make you wonder whether we're not back in the boom times. But everyone knows that all a traffic jam means is that a petrol station is open.

I tried to go to the mechanic's today to have him look at my car, which has been making a strange noise near the left wheel. Up to Sin el Fil the traffic was moving fast, then suddenly, starting at the bridge over the Salome roundabout, there was a bottleneck. The traffic slowed down, then stopped. After half an hour I had only managed to get off the bridge. In other words, I hadn't moved more than a hundred yards. After another half hour I decided to turn around, and slowly made my way back to the Salome roundabout. For more than an hour I'd been driving at walking speed, and soon the first queues appeared, endless lines of stopped cars, waiting, causing pile-ups and paralysing traffic. The drivers sat there for hours under the beating sun. Some left their cars to go and sit in the shade, or chat with other drivers. Apparently, there are queues that form in the middle of the night. The drivers claim their place in the queue, then leave their vehicles and come back in the early hours of the morning. After driving past two hundred, three hundred, four hundred waiting vehicles, I finally reached the petrol station, then drove past it, and the traffic moved freely again.

These petrol stations have become the most hated places in the country, but they are also the space where everyone's desires converge. A huge crowd gathers around each of these black holes in a failing world: countless employees, courier drivers, middlemen and the military charged with maintaining a semblance of discipline, hundreds of little delivery mopeds that don't have to respect the queues and crowd around the pumps. In the midst of all this commotion, the drivers whose turn it is to fill up can only advance with difficulty. The tension between the exasperated drivers, the holders of priority cards and the exhausted security is palpable. You get the sense that everything could blow up at any moment, and indeed, there have been numerous incidents. Now a kind of sinister aura has formed around the petrol stations, an aura of febrile agitation and foreboding.

14

The street trader walks by at the same time every day, singing the same song, an incomprehensible chant alerting us to his passage. He passes under my terrace and stops a little further on, where four or five old men from the neighbourhood are in the habit of gathering to talk and drink coffee. One of them brings it down from his kitchen on a pewter tray, the coffee pot steaming in the middle of a sundry collection of little cups. The men sit on plastic chairs and discuss everything, with great assurance. A couple of them appear more authoritative than the others, one of them is always smoking a cheap cigar, which must give him confidence. They talk about the economic situation, obviously, the shortages, the electricity rationing, the price of petrol on the black market. And then, gradually, they make their way back to politics, to the balance of international powers, the Americans, the Russians, the Iranians, the Chinese, who are all in cahoots, bringing us down while furthering their own interests. And then of course they move on to the local leaders, who are manipulating events to their own advantage, but whose failings are accepted as an inescapable fate, a force of nature like an earthquake, or a volcanic eruption. I doubt these men took part in any of the demonstrations in 2019.

The street trader stops his cart between two parked cars and hesitantly approaches the circle. He is familiar with this pavement conference, which he attends each time he passes. He, also, is probably convinced that he is held hostage to the incomprehensible designs of the great men of the age. And he, also, must see the incompetence and corruption of the country's leaders as a constant force beyond his control. He stays for five or ten minutes, leaning against his cart, on which an old washing machine and a rusty iron window frame are enthroned. He crosses his legs, his torso swaying slightly, his arms alongside his body, in the posture of a Greek statue.

15

Saad Hariri, the prime minister-designate, has stepped down without forming a cabinet. It took the ruling oligarchy months to name him as prime minister, which they did despite the fact that he had been booted out by the uprising of 17 October. Najib Mikati, his successor, is nominated to the post even though he was holding it the year the deadly ship with its cargo of ammonium nitrate entered the port of Beirut. He is not able to put together a cabinet either. President Aoun is getting in everyone's way. They are all squabbling about positions, everyone wanting a share of what is left, like vultures fighting over a corpse under the watchful eye of the armed militia.

16

My wife's hairdresser keeps ruminating about the problems with petrol. It's become an obsession for him, he spends all his time trying to devise stratagems to fill up his tank and his wife's; he's always looking for black-market salesmen, sending us messages to announce that he's found a station that will sell you petrol if you come late at night, and that he is prepared to help, or else he'll regale us with tales of his own prowess at the pumps, how he managed to leave his car at the station in the middle of the night so that he was the first one served when he came back at dawn. My wife Nayla, who is a psychotherapist, finally explained that this obsessive preoccupation with fuel was a defence mechanism, a way of distracting him from more serious anxieties, no doubt connected to the economy and the drastic fall of his living standards, his worry over his wife being pregnant in these difficult times when it's hard to find baby formula, and his hesitation about accepting an offer of employment in the Gulf states, which would compel him to leave his wife and not see his child grow up.

17

I've noticed that the greengrocers are not coming round any more. Up until a month ago one of them used to pass by with his overloaded cart. Unlike the street trader, the greengrocer had a stentorian voice and would articulate superbly, singing little rhyming couplets with imagery and a modulation at the end of each verse, lauding the qualities of his tomatoes, his oranges or his walnuts. The sight of the mountains of glowing fruit was irresistible. When someone called down from a balcony, he would stop dead, trying to bring his cart to a halt, but it would drag him along before he could bring it under control. I always used to buy something from him, it didn't matter what, just for the joy of seeing him work his old scales – placing the weights on the tray and swapping them around, those same gestures that his peers and predecessors have been using since I was a kid – with the lucid awareness that I was observing an immemorial human activity.

To my great satisfaction I found him back again this morning as I was coming home from an errand, his cart parked under the large bougainvillea and his eyes on his phone. His wares were not as attractive as they once were: there was less fruit, and the crates were not as full. I asked him if the news was good. After greeting me with a wide smile, he said no, his father had died in Turkey, and that's when I found out that he came from a village near Raqqa, that his entire family was in a Turkish refugee camp, and that they couldn't return home to Syria because one of his brothers had briefly fought against the regime. Their fields of olive trees had probably been burned by the soldiers because of this, along with their house. He showed me videos of charred tree trunks on his phone, footage taken by one of his cousins. I asked him how his work here was going, what with the economic crisis. He replied that everything had become so expensive that the operation was no longer viable, he was losing customers and couldn't even pay for the rental of his little cart. After a while he said that he was planning to leave Lebanon, but that he knew if he left he would never be able to come back. I sensed that he was about to say more, and waited, but he didn't add anything else.

Last week, Ronald told me that the tenant farmer he employs in the mountains had been preparing to leave for months, too, that he had been in contact with people smugglers in Tripoli, and that he had plans to go to Cyprus, then to Greece and on to Germany. But the last few months' inflation had reduced his salary to almost nothing. He couldn't even put enough money aside to pay the smugglers, and finally had to give up on the idea. As I was talking with my greengrocer, I fleetingly thought that he must be in the same fix, but I didn't say anything for fear of embarrassing him. While we were talking I jubilantly smelled some bunches of fresh mint. That smell was one of the first to disappear when my rhinitis came back. Before leaving the greengrocer I wanted to buy something, and I chose some greengage plums. They were beautiful but incredibly expensive. The greengrocer encouraged me to taste one. I was afraid I wouldn't be able to taste anything as I bit into the plum, but I only had to wait a second for its musky, powerful sweetness to spread through my mouth, like a delicate miracle.

18

The caretaker of our building and his wife asked to speak to me. They were sitting in our living room, ill at ease, and finally they told us the reason for their anxiety. They had been bearing up under the blows of the economic crisis without complaining much, but now their salary is worth almost nothing, and their living costs have risen so high that they are thinking of going back home to Sri Lanka. Their plan was to work hard here so that they could save enough to buy a small piece of land south of Colombo, where they would build a house for their children and have a roof over their heads in their old age. In order to do that they took a loan from a bank in Sri Lanka, but for a year now they haven't been able to make the repayment of a hundred dollars a month. That is now the equivalent of their entire salary, which doesn't even cover their daily expenses. Their fear is that they might have to sell the land, and that all their hard work over the last ten years will have been in vain. This story is similar to that of thousands of other immigrant workers, housekeepers, janitors and gardeners, who have been caught in the trap of Lebanon's economic crisis. It's strange to realise that the collapse of Lebanon has posed inextricable problems to families living at the other ends of the earth, in Colombo, Dhaka, Kathmandu and the outskirts of Addis Ababa.

19

The litany is endless, desperate: Beirut's public hospital has announced that it has only four more days' worth of fuel. The millers' trade union has issued a warning that soon mills will no longer be able to operate. The water company of Beirut and Mount Lebanon has announced that it will be starting a drastic rationing programme for water distribution.

20

We must try to live, said the poet Paul Valéry. This has become our principal occupation. Each in our own way, according to our means. We still go to the mountains, to our friends' gardens, or, in the evenings in Beirut, to houses that were blown up by the explosion and then rebuilt, where we talk about the economic crisis, always the crisis, despite the wine and the laughter. The day before yesterday we had dinner at Selim Mouzannar's house. There were about ten of us, including Karim Ben Cheikh, the Consul General of France, whose posting would end the following night. The conversation lingered on the best strategy to unify the opposition movements. But we also talked about Oman, where Karim is headed next because his wife has been named the ambassador there, and a former minister of culture told stories about the country from when his position allowed him to travel there frequently. From time to time, Selim would get up and play the piano in the middle of his large white living room. At one point someone told the story of the three bears that had been found abandoned in cages, malnourished and suffering psychologically, no doubt owned by a small-time zoo or a so-called animal lover. But they were the lucky ones: members of an international organisation had come to rescue them. They had fed them and cared for them, then evacuated them on huge stretchers, with the help of foreign volunteers, from the hell they had been living in. At around ten o'clock, the consul left because he had to meet his successor at the airport, and he made us promise to wait for him. We went out into the garden to smoke cigars, and at eleven the consul returned, unexpectedly accompanied by his successor and his wife. For the rest of the evening, I couldn't stop wondering how these two people would interpret the spectacle of this small gathering smoking cigars and drinking French wines, sitting in a deliciously scented garden beneath the floodlit facade of the house with its expanse of white marble flooring, when they had just driven across the dark city, its sinister streets like deep wells, a city in crisis.

We might well have given the impression of being like those Roman nobles in the last days of the empire, living in feigned indifference to their fate, to the collapse of the world they knew, to their ignorance of what would replace it, like Apronenia Avitia and her friends. But in truth, that's not what is happening. For the first time in our history, we are no longer in denial. Perhaps we are just trying to find a way of dealing with our powerlessness in the face of those who are letting the country go to rack and ruin. Or it's our way of defying the collapse, of resisting, still.

21

Some nights, the same thing seems to be happening on Badaro Street, where the cafes and bars are full to bursting, and the atmosphere is almost festive. The customers that cannot be seated in the cafes spill out onto the pavements, into the darkness of the street. And the laughter, the shouts and the noisy conversations seem to defy the blackness of the night.

In front of the cafes, as night falls, the queues of cars are already forming, waiting for the possibility of a petrol station opening the next day. The revellers lean against the vehicles, talking away, a glass in hand.

22

I go on foot to get my daughter, who is spending the evening with a friend in one of those bars. It is dark, and the streets are too deserted for it to be safe for her to walk home alone. As we walk, we pass by the busy, lit-up bars, whose front tables on the pavement seem to be set up at the edge of darkness, so stark is the division between the lights and the thick gloom of the unlit street. Whenever a car drives by, its headlights project giant dancing shadows and spectral forms onto the facades all around us.

On the edge of Sami el Solh avenue, I point to the clear sky, sparkling with stars as if we were out in the countryside, because of the lack of city lights. Saria takes out her phone and we try to identify the constellations with an app that shows them drawn on the screen when you point it up at the cosmos.

As we cross the deserted avenue, we see two peculiar and alarming individuals, one very tall and the other smaller, squat, limping slightly and holding a big stick, like a shepherd. They walk past without looking at us, as though absorbed in some internal drama. My daughter and I have the same bizarre impression, namely that these two beings are not in their rightful place, that we have perhaps just met two characters from another dimension, a fairy tale or a projection of the terror and magic of the deep night.

23

Yesterday around noon, on the same avenue, I saw a moped coming towards me, one of the thousands in the city these days. Its driver had a helmet – not on his head but hanging off the handlebars. As he approached, the helmet fell off and started rolling in parallel to the rider like a cheerful little dog, bouncing along the tarmac so quickly that it seemed to be racing the moped, and even overtook it just as they passed in front of me.

24

A few days ago a city dumpster was rolling by itself down a steep street. It moved with courtesy and caution, in a series of strange loops, avoiding all the parked cars, then bumped into the side of the pavement and tipped over, without causing any damage at all. ■

CONTRIBUTORS

Fatima Bhutto was born in Kabul, Afghanistan, and grew up in Syria and Pakistan. Her most recent writing includes the novel *The Runaways* and a non-fiction book about the changing world of global pop culture, *New Kings of the World*.

Chris Dennis is a writer and public health educator from southern Illinois. He is the author of *Here Is What You Do*. Other work has appeared in *Granta*, the *Paris Review, Playgirl, McSweeney's, Literary Hub* and *Guernica*. He holds a master's degree from Washington University in St Louis, where he also received a postgraduate fellowship.

Ruth Diver is the translator of Charif Majdalani's *Beirut 2020*. Her recent translations include *Arcadia* by Emmanuelle Bayamack-Tam, and *Maraudes* by Sophie Pujas, for which she won the 2016 *Asymptote* Close Approximations Fiction Prize.

Akwaeke Emezi is the author of the memoir *Dear Senthuran* and the novels *The Death of Vivek Oji, Freshwater* and *Pet*. In 2018, they were chosen as one of the National Book Foundation's 5 Under 35.

Janice Galloway is an award-winning author of short stories, novels and memoir, and has collaborated with composers and visual artists. Her latest book, *Jellyfish*, was published in 2019.

Nathan Harris is the author of *The Sweetness of Water*, which was longlisted for the Man Booker Prize, the Center for Fiction First Novel Prize and the Andrew Carnegie Medal for Excellence in Fiction. In 2021, he was chosen as one of the National Book Foundation's 5 Under 35.

Julie Hecht is the author of the story collections *Do the Windows Open?*, all first published in the *New Yorker*, and *Happy Trails to You*; the novel *The Unprofessionals*; and *Was This Man a Genius?: Talks with Andy Kaufman*. She has won an O. Henry Prize and a Guggenheim Fellowship. She is currently writing her next book, *Every Single Thing*.

The Herak family came to the UK in 2005. When asked why they came, they talk about the hope for a better life, and sparing their children the discrimination Roma people face in Slovakia.

Sheila Heti is the author of ten books, including the novels *Motherhood* and *How Should a Person Be?*. 'Pure Colour' is an excerpt from her novel of the same title, forthcoming from Farrar, Straus and Giroux in the US, Harvill Secker in the UK and Knopf in Canada.

Lewis Khan is a photographic artist from London, working with stills and moving image. His portrait-based work is a study of emotion, relationships and identity. His project *Theatre*, the result of a four-year residency in two London hospitals, was published by The Lost Light Recordings.

Damian Le Bas is a writer from Sussex, England. His first book, *The Stopping Places*, won the Somerset Maugham Award, a Jerwood Award and was shortlisted for the Stanford Dolman Travel Book of the Year. He read theology at St John's College, Oxford.

Rachel Long's debut collection, *My Darling from the Lions*, was shortlisted for the Forward Prize for Best First Collection and the Costa Poetry Award. She is the founder of the Octavia Poetry Collective for women of colour.

Moses McKenzie is of Jamaican heritage and grew up in Bristol, UK, where he still lives and writes full-time. 'An Olive Grove in Ends' is an excerpt from his debut novel of the same title, forthcoming from Wildfire in the UK and Little, Brown in the US.

Charif Majdalani is a Lebanese writer, novelist and professor. His books include *Moving the Palace*, translated by Edward Gauvin, and *Beirut 2020*, translated by Ruth Diver. He is a member of the *L'Orient littéraire*'s editorial board and president of the International Writers' House in Beirut.

Will Rees is a writer and editor living in London. He is a director of Peninsula Press, which he co-founded in 2018. He is currently working on his first book, a cultural essay about hypochondria.

Claire Schwartz is the author of the forthcoming poetry collection *Civil Service* and the poetry editor of *Jewish Currents*. She lives in Brooklyn, New York.

Debbie Urbanski's stories and essays have been published in the *Best American Science Fiction and Fantasy*, the *Best American Experimental Writing* and the *Sun*, a magazine based in North Carolina. Her first novel, *What Comes After the End*, will be published in 2023.

Dawn Watson is a writer from Belfast. Her debut poetry pamphlet, *The Stack of Owls is Getting Higher*, was published in 2019. She has been published in journals including the *Manchester Review*, the *Moth*, *Blackbox Manifold* and the *Stinging Fly*.

Kate Zambreno is the author, most recently, of *Drifts* and *To Write as if Already Dead*, a study of Hervé Guibert. She is a 2021 Guggenheim Fellow, and is at work on a non-fiction book, *The Light Room*, and a story collection, *The Missing Person*.

Give the gift of Membership

Set someone special on a journey through human history. They'll enjoy 12 months of extraordinary exhibitions as well as an exclusive programme of Membership events.

Buy now

Ways to buy
britishmuseum.org/membership
+44 (0)20 7323 8195

Large vase, tin-glazed earthenware (maiolica), from the workshop of Orazio Fontana, made in Urbino, Italy, about 1565–1571, with gilt-metal mounts made in Paris, France, about 1765. Part of the Waddesdon Bequest.